black AMERICAN MONEY

How black Power Can Thrive in a Capitalist Society

Dr. Boyce Watkins

Blue Boy Publishing Co.
Camillus, NY

Dr. Boyce Watkins

Dr. Boyce Watkins is a Finance Professor at Syracuse University and resident Scholar for AOL black Voices. He is also a key contributor to MSNBC's TheGrio.com and founder of the Your Black World Coalition. For more information about Dr. Watkins and his work, please visit www.BoyceWatkins.com.

Dr. Boyce Watkins

Copyright © 2009 by Dr. Boyce Watkins
All rights reserved.

Published by

Blue Boy Publishing Co.
PO Box 691
Camillus, NY 13031-0691

Printed in the United States of America
Cover designed by Glenda Warren Yancey

First printing, October 2009

Library of Congress Catalog-in-
Publications Data

black American Money, 1st ed.

p.cm.

ISBN: 0-9742632-8-1
Library of Congress Control Number:

Disclaimer

All statements made in this book are matters of social commentary and opinion. All facts stated are verified with the most reliable sources available. Neither the author nor the publisher assumes responsibility for errors.

This book is dedicated to my daughters, Thaiiesha, Carmen and Patrice. Also, to my son David – I pray that one day we see each other again.

I would also like to thank my parents, Robin and Larry, for their love and support. My brother Lawrence has been loyal through the tough times and congratulations to my sister Latanja for finishing medical school. I know what you went through to get there, which is part of the reason I respect you so much.

Mostly, I'd like to thank my assistant, Shauntay Prewitt, for putting up with the stress of working with me. I'd also like to express my appreciation to Diana Atkinson, Tarin Donatien, Jazelle Reed, Shanelle Walker and Tiffany Brown for working hard on my behalf. Thanks to my entire team, I'd be nothing without you.

I would finally like to thank the 30,000 plus members of the Your Black World Coalition and others across the world who've shown support for my career in public scholarship. The hurdles are great, but our vision is greater. We are meant to be successful.

Contents

Introduction

I should begin by saying that I am not a Finance Professor who happens to be black. Rather, I am a black man who happens to be a Finance Professor. The goal of this work was not to create yet another book analyzing money to the nth degree, discussing stocks, bonds, charts and portfolios. While I've done exhaustive research on such matters and made a multitude of purely financial media appearances, I see money in an admittedly broad and inclusive framework. Personally, I see money as a tool for the enhancement of life and the liberation of a people. It can also be a weapon for the destruction of life and the enslavement of people. Finally, I see money as part of a nexus of critical issues that drive the world in which we live. How we process and harness the power of money plays a crucial role in our personal and collective outcomes.

This book is not going to be about money throughout. It does not contain a long list of "nuts and bolts" financial advisories, "dos and don'ts" or technical trading rules. It is a discussion, by a black social commentator who cares about America. One who also happens to be an educator and financial expert. So, imagine a person who enjoys cooking steak, chicken and carrots, but insists upon making sure the plate has a little bit of each. I have never been one dimensional in my analysis, because linear, limited thinking can cause one to consistently miss the big picture. Unfortunately, such is the limitation of many American academics, most of who are trained to focus on one tiny area of research, presuming that the world can be understood with constrained, one dimensional, half-baked understanding. I will always feel that this viewpoint is incorrect.

In this book, you are going to get first hand views on how money plays a role in critical black issues and leadership, from The State of the black Union to Civil Rights. I will openly and honestly share my behind-the-scenes experiences with CNN, FOX, ESPN and other networks. You will hear about academia, as I take you on a quick trip into the ivory tower for a discussion of how economic incentives impact the value systems of today's "blackademics". We will discuss how millions of members of the black Middle Class, by neglecting the significance of ownership, have transformed themselves into high paid sharecroppers. Finally, we will discuss the Great Financial Crisis of 2009, what went wrong and why it was unlike any other. The trip will be long and broad, and won't just focus on money. Rather, the focus is on building capital of all types, not just financial capital.

Money, like any other powerful object, can either be incredibly constructive or horrifically destructive. It can ruin families or make people strong. It can liberate, enslave and do everything in between. You can improve the lives of those you love or ruin important relationships. Money can do many amazing things in a capitalist society. Therefore, understanding, embracing and controlling the power of money is clearly, without question, an undeniably meaningful part of the movement toward equal rights.

Chapter 1

What I learned from the Nappy Headed Hoe

As I write these words, my mind takes me to another place and time. It was an early and tiring Sunday morning, and I'd been up late working the night before. I received a call from Stacey, a producer with The Jesse Jackson Show, who also happens to be a dear friend. She mentioned that they needed me on the radio immediately and that the topic of conversation was a guy named Don Imus.

I'd only heard about Imus a few days earlier. Don Imus was a radio "shock jock" at MSNBC, who decided that the women from the Rutgers University basketball team, mostly black, were a pack of "Nappy headed hoes". Why a man with a predominantly white audience would choose those words to describe women on a basketball team was beyond me. I use slang when I speak, but only with those who understand what the hell it is I am saying. I am not sure if the predominantly white, conservative audience of Don Imus would even be able to get a laugh out of his disgusting and risky statement.

Imus' words sparked a national controversy. The comment led to yet another one of those artificial conversations on race that spontaneously combusts when something happens to remind us how little we've traveled down the road toward serious and solid race relations.

1

Whites and blacks have spent 400 years learning how to not get along with one another. Black people have learned to survive in complete and total fear of white America, muting our voices when it is time for our voices to be heard. Even saying and doing the right thing becomes relative and subjective under the watchful and overbearing eye of those who hate us. This is not to say that whites are mean people, it is to say that this form of cultural domination keeps individuals even as powerful as Barack Obama from using the words "black man" in public (try to think about the last time you heard President Obama use those words).

I asked Stacey, the producer, if there would be another person on the phone with myself and Rev. Jackson. She said "You'll be on with Rev. Al Sharpton."

"Oh, okay," I said.

I'd been on several shows with Al Sharpton in the past, and I've always found him to be an interesting man. No one mobilizes black people better than Al and if there were ever a black man who struck fear in the establishment, it would be him. I also learned to be mindful of just how closely aligned I became with Al, since I don't always agree with his views. At the same time, it is our diversity of viewpoints that allows us to support one another. As a professor, I have always agreed with Rev. Sharpton's perspective that black scholars don't do enough to help the black community. As a pastor and Civil Rights leader, Rev. Sharpton understands my critique regarding the need for black leaders to listen to younger voices in the black community.

I eventually became a weekly commentator on Rev. Sharpton's radio show, and it quickly became my favorite media appearance each week. We would discuss serious issues, but we would also have fun. It's the ability to have fun while fighting for justice that makes me appreciate my time with Reverend Al.

Being a believer in free speech, I had objections to what I perceived to be Rev. Sharpton's argument that it should be illegal to use the word "nigger" in public. Being called a "nigger" means you need to get pimp slapped and beat down, not arrested. Finally, I parted with Al during the case of football star Michael Vick, who was accused of dog fighting, sent to prison and vilified by the American public. Al took the side of PETA (People for the Ethical Treatment of Animals) who worked overtime to throw Michael Vick under the bus. I personally felt that Vick made a terrible mistake, but that as a young man, he should eventually be given the right to play football again and repair his broken life.

Although I would have supported Al Sharpton and Rev. Jackson in past presidential elections (had they received the Democratic nomination), I quietly fear the day that any pastor is to become president. There is a reason church and state should be separated. The mind of the religious figure can sometimes be riddled with a powerful self-righteousness that can only be bestowed by a higher power. This problematic monopoly on the truth can sometimes lead one to believe that individual liberties should be put to the wayside in favor of a more paternalistic dictatorship and absolute control over human choice and condition. Every pimp in America controls his employees by presuming that he knows what's best for them, and there are honestly quite a few pimps in the pulpit. One hundred years after electing your first religious figure into the white House, you become another Iran.

3

The conversation with Jesse and Al over the Don Imus situation was as interesting to listen to as it was to participate. I did not feel compelled to speak more than necessary, since I have tremendous respect for Reverends Sharpton and Jackson as veterans of American civil rights. At the same time, I felt it necessary to inject a fresh, youthful, scholarly and practical voice into the conversation, as there are times when being perched high on the tree can lead one to see a reality that is simply not in sync with the common man and woman. I've always worked hard to be a man of the people, so I listen to people to learn what they are thinking.

Jesse and Al had solutions to the Imus problem that were tried, true and effective. As men of action, Revs Sharpton and Jackson had planned protests around the country to challenge MSNBC for their support of Don Imus. Black public scholars are good at talking, but not so good at actually following through with meaningful action. We are trained by academia that if you talk about something long enough, it will eventually change itself. While there is certainly room for intellectual leadership, we must be sure that words are followed by activity, or the words get lost in the wind. At the very least, scholars should provide action plans to the community that will turn our instructions into reality.

Although I respected Al and Jesse's plans for protest, my mind went in other directions. One thing I know about MSNBC, or any news organization, is that they are, first and foremost, a CORPORATION. Knowing how corporations think and what makes them tick is exactly how you gain the ability to stab the dragon in the heart.

I knew that when it came to how Don Imus was viewed by his colleagues, race was almost entirely secondary in their perception of him. Imus' supporters didn't back him because he was another white man. They didn't like him because he wore a cowboy hat or had a really great show. They liked Don Imus...in fact, loved him, for one reason: He was a money-maker.

The heads of major media organizations revel in the fact that Imus can connect them with a sellable product (his audience), which makes them pay Imus large sums of money to host their shows.

The system works well, as long as it's working. Media is not about entertainment. It is about *making money for Corporate America.* If you stop the flow of money, you stop the flow of power.

On the radio with Rev. Sharpton and Rev. Jackson, I was thinking out loud on ways to make sure the system stopped working. I mentioned one simple reality to Jesse and Al: Any white man will abandon another white man if he is no longer making money. The same is true for African-Americans, Asians and other ethnic groups.

When comparing a major media outlet to the drug game, one additional truth is that becoming a problem will get you "whacked". Many drug murders do not occur because of one person gets angry at another.   They occur because of a conflict of interest. For thousands of years, men have killed their friends due to conflicts of interest. Well, women have too, but you get the point.

I mentioned that if we get to the bottom of the Don Imus "paper trail" (his source of income), we could have some impact on his job security. The key was not to go after Imus. It was also not to go after MSNBC. It was to go after his CORPORATE SPONSORS. Getting to the financial root of the issue was the key in all this.

Along with making a profit, corporate sponsors must answer to those from whom they are making their money, the consumer. If the consumer is not happy with the nature of the medium through which corporations are delivering their messages, they may no longer be willing to purchase their products. Most consumers pay little attention to a show's list of corporate sponsors. However, highlighting that list might bring problems for the company if their hosts are engaged in controversial behavior.

One way I knew we could turn off some of the Don Imus corporate sponsors was by relying on America's disdain for obvious racism. Americans don't like the idea of racism, especially what I call "first-grader" racism, which usually comes in the most blatant form. "First grader" racism is direct, good old fashioned racial hate; the kind that rarely occurs in today's society. However, stomping out the first grader racism is what makes Americans feel that they are doing something important.

Examples of first grader racism might include the following:
1) Hearing someone use the word "nigger"

2) Someone joining the skinheads, Neo-Nazis or the Ku Klux Klan

3) Someone hanging a noose on his neighbor's front door.

4) Someone admitting that they do not like black people because they are black.

5) Anyone in the South who puts the Confederate Flag on the back of his or her truck (we all know that only people from the south can be racist, right?).

Although most Americans hate the idea of racism, they are quite ready and willing to keep the practice of racial exclusion alive. Americans won't agree with Imus using terms like "Nappy Headed Hoe", but they will certainly applaud the likes of Bill O'Reilly and Sean Hannity, who spout incredibly racist rhetoric week after week.

Many Americans are the first to attack those who use the word "nigger", but they are the last to challenge the prison system and its Jim Crow-like incarceration of millions of black men.

Americans are quick to go after the skinhead and boo him on Jerry Springer, but they are the last to show any concern for the fact that most universities in America have at least 20 or 30 academic departments that have never tenured (or even hired) a black faculty member in over 100 years of existence.

Many Americans think that electing a president who is 50% black implies that racism is dead and buried and that there is no need for leadership within the black community. Such values remind us that when it comes to race and racism, America clearly needs to learn a few lessons.

That is the great American Hypocrisy when it comes to race. What is most interesting is that there are times when this hypocrisy can be used as a weapon to cue up social norms to help your cause. Most Americans believe they are not racist, so it's easy to get them to mobilize against blatant racism. The tradeoff is that there is a tremendous backlash when you work to get America to confront the subtle, damaging and poisonous venom of institutionalized racial inequality.

7

The Don Imus situation was, relatively speaking, a slam dunk. Even people with little understanding of racism were made uncomfortable by the term "Nappy headed hoe." Of course there are those in the Right Wing (and black commentators paid to support their rhetoric) who will defend nearly any vile thing that anyone says about black people. But in this case, they were in the minority. I explained to Jesse and Al that if they simply put Imus' sponsors on the spot, they could get Imus off the air. Corporations are, by definition, relatively conservative and completely disinterested in even the slightest bit of controversy. The show with Jesse and Al lasted an hour, and at that time, I had no idea that this was going to be the biggest news story of the month, and perhaps even the entire year.

A few days later, when I saw Jesse and Al holding a press conference, I listened carefully to their words. Even though they'd implemented my idea of going after Imus' corporate sponsors, they didn't mention my name. That was actually for the best, since I've often felt that my university hates me enough for speaking out on issues of race. It amazes me that many northeastern campuses claim to embrace liberal thought, but even they break and bend the rules of free expression when it comes to black issues. The disease of racism affects us all, and it has its greatest impact on those who think they've been cured.

Soon after our conversation on the radio, the strategy of going after the corporate sponsors of Don Imus and his Show started to work. Once I heard that one of Imus' major sponsors had jumped ship, I knew he was done. The other predictable element of American behavior is the Band Wagon Effect. When one major individual or group agrees or disagrees with an idea, the rest of the world can easily end up following suit. This effect is especially strong among risk-averse corporations, who avoid controversy whenever possible. After the first major sponsor or two stepped out on Imus, the rest of them ran screaming. At that point, Imus was off the air.

The most interesting part of the Don Imus case was that Imus was put back on the air just a few months later. Executives behind closed doors likely told Imus to "let those people calm down and we'll get you right back." The same was true for Dog the Bounty Hunter, a character on the cable channel A&E, who was found to have liberally referred to his son's black girlfriend as "that nigger" several times during a long telephone conversation. I heard the conversation, and he wasn't using the word "nigger" in any way other than its worst intent.

Soon after Dog the Bounty Hunter was removed from the air, A&E attempted to put him back on television. I recall doing a lot of interviews about Dog, and our Youtube.com video on the topic received thousands of views. I received over 1,000 emails on the topic, begging me to forgive Dog for his behavior and reminding me that all people make mistakes. While I agree that everyone makes mistakes, I believe that if Dog the Bounty Hunter had been a black man on a white network making the same error, he would have been blackballed forever. Like Dog The Bounty Hunter, Don Imus also received a second chance after his egregious and insulting mistake.

Additionally, while Imus was so easily forgiven and given another chance, many of these networks have rarely, if ever, given a single chance to any African-American host to grace their airwaves. I wasn't sure why one would further the idea of giving an old boring guy another chance when there are so many interesting people of color willing to do a great job.

The experiences of Dog the Bounty Hunter and Don Imus were great reminders of the following truisms about America:

America is a capitalist country.
America is more capitalist than it is racist.
America is more capitalist than it is sexist.
America is more capitalist than it is homophobic.
America is more capitalist than it is democratic.

I agree with the late great actor Ozzie Davis who said, "America will forgive you for being black, but it will never forgive you for being poor."

You can be a lot of things in America, but having the right amount of money trumps nearly everything. Even President Bush, a cowboy from Texas, would embrace the gayest, blackest, woman on earth if she had enough money in her pocket. Capitalism is America's building block and also the ultimate trump card.

In America, money overrules nearly every value system we hold dear. Prestigious academic institutions across America pimp themselves out to television networks and regularly accept unqualified students in order to make money through NCAA sports. Politicians regularly sell out the American people to special interest groups who bring enough cash to the table. Baptist ministers were bought out with faith-based funding during the 2004 Presidential election. Otherwise repulsive men become "woman magnets" if one part of their body is massive enough: their wallet. So yes, size really DOES matter in relationships.

Human beings need resources. In America, a country that has been eaten alive by its excesses, the need to obtain the financial drug that keeps us high is both alarming and perpetual. Americans under save, under invest, overspend and over borrow. All of this behavior is fueled by VH-1 episodes that make us want to live like Paris Hilton.

It's too bad that Martin Luther King was not a Finance Professor. If only he'd had a financial expert next to him during his movement, he might have come to understand the missing, yet most critical element of his drive toward equality. Martin Luther King was a fearless man who realized that African-Americans may have been poor in cash, but wealthy in faith. Faith in God is what keeps people moving, even when they are weary and weak. It is what allows you to look in the face of any obstacle and realize that there is light at the end of the tunnel, even when you've seen certified reports stating that the tunnel is dark from beginning to end.

Beyond our tremendous faith, we all need liberation from the thing we fear most: Not being able to provide for our families. Many powerful movements in the black community started with great ideas and a large amount of spirit. Through time, however, many movements died because the life-sustaining force of resource acquisition and allocation was not part of the movement's infrastructure.

"I would keep going, but I got bills to pay," says the former activist, who now takes a full-time job with IBM and can no longer work with the community center.

"I used to wanna keep it real, but now I have to keep it REALISTIC," says the student who takes the corporate job after college, cuts off her dreadlocks and only uses "radical black language" when she is at home at the dinner table.

"If we keep acting this way, we are going to ruin our careers," says the doctor, lawyer, or professor in graduate school, who fears speaking out against blatant injustice in the workplace.

If you ever want to know why someone does something you don't understand, the money trail is a good place to start. If you want to figure out why politicians make laws that their constituents clearly don't support, find out who is giving them money. Everything from why a hooker hooks to why an attorney represents a child molester almost always connects to money.

Given that many human incentives usually have a paper trail, it is critical to understand how these trails work. One must know how to sniff them out and analyze the paper trail of others, while being mindful of your own. Once you've determined your own paper trail, it becomes critical to learn how to dictate and create the kind of paper trail that will create the right incentives for you. It's much easier to do the right thing when you are not being penalized for doing so.

Chapter 2

Had I Marched with Dr. King

I never had a chance to march with Dr. King. There are some older leaders in the black community who almost make this a liability when a young scholar attempts to speak on social movements. But I've had a chance to interact extensively with some of our black leaders, and I respect them quite a bit.

Dr. King did an extraordinary job for the time in which he lived. The idea of wealth building was remote when considering the fact that there were few significant sources of income to speak of. Black folks had to get jobs before they could build wealth from the income being provided by those jobs. Dr. King's work had an amazing, powerful and impactful purpose, and without such work, none of us would have the opportunities that we have today.

One challenge of most social movements is that we tend to move forward by reaching into whatever toolkit we have at our disposal. For example, teachers may have a tendency to see education as the solution to many problems. Doctors see healthcare as a pressing concern. Financial people see money as a critical issue. Pastors turn to the great power of the church in their quest for advancement.

Dr. King, being a pastor, was obviously going to turn first and foremost to the church to provide the spiritual and social strength necessary to sustain his movement. He was right to turn to the church, because the black church is one of the most powerful unifying forces in the black community. It is clearly our rock, our foundation, the place where no one dares to mess with us.

Had I marched with Dr. King, I would have brought in a team of powerful financial advisors to supplement his movement. The advisors would have laid out strategies for African-American wealth building, saving, investing and entrepreneurship. The goal of integration would have become secondary to a more important goal: integration on the right terms. One does not want to integrate into a financial powerhouse as a consumer. Doing so does not promote wealth building, power, freedom or equality. Integration as a consumer and worker relegates one to being a cog on the giant wheel of corporate America.

Corporate America needs its consumers in the same way a dope dealer needs his addicts. Black Americans have historically been the consumers of American products, never invited to the table of decision makers, shareholders, and corporate titans. At the same time, we have not worked very hard to demand a seat at the table. Our culture is one that breeds consumerism as the first objective, as our kids are quick to demand the latest pair of Air Jordans, the nicest outfits, or the newest and cleanest car on the block. They are not much different from white kids, however. The only difference is that white American youth tend to have a cushion of wealth on which to build their futures, as well as a different brand of financial literacy taught in the home. The tradition of simple ownership via purchasing your own home, buying stocks, and investing in the 401k is instilled in white children much more readily than children of color.

African-Americans have also integrated themselves into the American dream as workers. We have been the hardest workers in America for the past 400 years. There is no greater commitment to America than having worked for hundreds of years without compensation. America was built on the backs of black Americans, and even to this day, we stand supporting a long list of politicians who are completely unwilling to even apologize for slavery, let alone secure fair compensation.

When I go to "the hood" to speak to youth about economic and educational empowerment, I see a lot of kids who know how to work hard. They have been indoctrinated into a world of manual labor, one that pays minimum wage in exchange for long, tiring days and a bad back. I feel bad for many of them, as I think "If you only knew. If you only realized that this is exactly what the world wants from you. If you only realized that you can work half as hard to get twice as much if you simply put yourself in the right circumstances."

Everything in life is about context. If you want to kill people, you shouldn't become a hit man, because you'll probably go to prison. Instead, you become a soldier, where you'll get medals for shooting others. If you want to work 14 hours a day, you don't become a manual laborer to get minimum wage. You become an attorney or a doctor, and earn 100 times that amount.

I've met many black geniuses who use their genius to navigate the penitentiary, which takes far more intelligence than it does to navigate even the most prestigious and powerful universities. If only they understood context and the importance of putting your skills to work in the right scenarios.

Black people are trained to be laborers. The greatest indication of where a man ends up is usually where he started. A large percentage of our outcome is statistically determined the day we arrive on this earth, especially if we are heavily influenced by those in our family who've come before us. Our world view can become quite limited on the very day we are born.

Black children are not the only ones with a limited world view. Kids from the suburbs are the same way. The kid who grew up in Bel Air (a wealthy neighborhood in California) is not likely to want to expand outside his comfortable surroundings. The difference is that resources are already nearby from the time he enters the world and he does not have to leave his surroundings to obtain them. Black youth, in order to obtain resources and experience the richness of America, find themselves forced to leave their environments to do so.

Had I marched with Dr. King, I would have thought carefully about how integration could proceed without cultural dilution. I would have promoted a discussion about capitalism in America and how integration without power leads to enslavement in a capitalist society. A woman who convinces an abusive boyfriend to marry her is only signing on for more abuse. After the wedding, rather than simply neglecting her and beating her when he comes to visit, she now sits in the home with him every day and is beaten on a regular basis. If her husband is wealthy, the wife is given access to a comfortable home and the best amenities, yet consistently reminded that she owns nothing. She is reminded that she is only allowed to enjoy the home out of the goodness of her oppressive husband's heart.

He loves his spouse, even when he beats her. He expects her to be grateful for the fact that he has allowed her to share this wonderful life with him. And now that she is in the home, in the marriage, she cannot leave the abuse so easily. Any decision to disconnect, even to regain her psychological footing, is interpreted as a lack of commitment to the marriage. At the end of the day, she realizes that she signed a very bad deal.

Black America, through integration, signed what some might consider a terrible deal. We signed on for cultural and economic interaction that led to dilution and powerlessness. The abusive spouse chose to marry us because we demanded it. And once the marriage occurred, divorce has not been an option. Any effort to regain our strength by coming together to support other black people is considered unpatriotic or "divisive."

We are cogs in the wheel of capitalism. We are the laborers and the consumers, not the owners and decision-makers. We signed a marriage certificate to a society that will not allow us to leave the house and has relegated us to a more consistent form of second-class citizenship. What is most horrific about this existence is that *we asked for it*. Like the abused woman with low self-esteem who so dearly wants to marry her abusive boyfriend, we got the wedding certificate, but only on his terms. Perhaps it's time to renegotiate the deal. But this requires an understanding of America and its systems, and goes beyond celebrating symbolic achievements, like having a black president. It requires us to think about the masses of black people and how we can aim our minds toward prosperity and success. It requires a *revolution*. This revolution might very likely be televised and even on the Internet. It's time to change the game.

Chapter 3

Where I came from

I have, perhaps by choice of a higher power, had a unique opportunity to experience nearly every dimension of the black male experience. I was almost shot; I've turned down scholarships to Ivy League schools; I've come close to going to jail; I've taught courses in foreign countries; I was born in the projects; I've done social commentary in front of millions of people; I've been fired from my job; I've rubbed elbows with multi-millionaires and even taught them a thing or two about money. I've had a chance to do it all.

From the top to the bottom and everything in between, I've had the chance to experience the richness of America. I've also had a chance to go face-to-face with the horror of being a black man in America. This unique set of experiences fueled my passion for providing perspective on various segments of American society in our nation's on-going racial dialogue. Most of us never leave the social class from which we came. We are, therefore, unable to empathize with those of a different background. I've risen through the ranks of America's social order and kept a desire to maintain my connection with my people. This has served as both an asset and a liability throughout my career.

My mother got pregnant with me when she was 16 years old. My father, a 15-year-old boy, wasn't quite interested in being a father. I can't say I blame him, as 15-year-olds are pretty much children themselves. From the minute he heard that the pregnancy test was positive, he ran in the other direction, at least that's my mom's side of the story. I recall my mother once explaining to me what it's like to have someone you love tell you they just don't want to be bothered with you anymore. I sensed there is pain in her heart from that experience, but we've never had the chance to really dig into what happened. Ironically, I would go through a similar experience at the age of 18, when the mother of my child would leave me for another man.

My grandmother put my mother out of the house when she gave birth to me, so my mother and I lived in the projects together. When I was 3-years-old, my mother met another young man and chose to marry him. So, there we were: this happy little black family without a pot to piss in (excuse my French).

I have never referred to this man (Larry Watkins) as my stepfather, and I honestly didn't know he wasn't my real father until I was 10 years old. I never wondered why he had light skin and I didn't. I also never wondered why women swooned over him, but girls have never swooned over me. I just assumed that God decided to curse me by letting the good genes skip right over my head. Either way, he was my dad....nothing less. I will always love him for his sacrifice.

My father was a Vietnam vet who eventually became a police officer. He was violent, mean, strong and proud. I assume things could have been worse, because a lot of black men came back from Vietnam in a box or on drugs. I am not quite sure if my father tried any of the drugs in Vietnam. If he did, he was never hamstrung by any form of addiction. He saw addiction as a weakness, and I only recall his brief fight with alcohol later in life, a fight that he won with flying colors. Although my dad was a violent man, he was the kind of man who would be willing to be violent to protect his family. So, I would describe him as more of an aggressive protector than a frightening victimizer.

My father taught me to be strong, focused and powerful in my approach to the world. If I were to give him a motto, it would be "just do it God damn it." My father was no loser, he was no-nonsense, and he was about business. When I am operating at my best, I can be the same way.

I wish my father had spent more time with me, but like most 20-somethings, he was into himself. He even admitted that men shouldn't have kids or get married until their 30s, because they are too selfish when they are young. Even as a child, I presumed that a 20-something year old man would surely have better things to do than spend all his time raising a child that wasn't even his own. I see parenting as a job that is almost never perfectly done, and in the end, you simply hope that the good outweighs the bad. In my case, the good experiences overcame the bad ones, so everything turned out alright.

Speaking to my father, or having him speak back to me, was an honor. I could never relate to those kids who became best buddies with their dad. I didn't have the kind of father who came home each day and said "I love you son". I never knew direct love from my dad, but I knew he cared. Again, I was practical, so I figured that if you come home every night and pay the bills on time, you probably give a damn.

My mother was the first to realize that I might end up with a career in social commentary and activism. She learned very early that I had a huge intolerance for injustice. It started with little things, like the outrage I might express at my being falsely accused of eating the rest of the peanut butter. I would plead with my mother to understand that I was innocent, even when I was no longer in danger of being punished. Then, there would be the threat of getting a "whoopin" if I didn't shut up. But, in spite of the threats, there was always something inside me that had to make sure the truth got out. No matter the consequence, the pain of holding back in the face of injustice would eat at me until I had to open my mouth. Even with the pain of getting slapped, I was still satisfied that truth and justice had been served.

My mother, noticing my inability to remain silent in the face of unfairness, would say "Boy, your mouth is either going to make you great or get you killed, I'm curious to see which one." Years later, seeing her son speaking truth to power in front of millions of people on CNN, my mom realized that she was the first witness to something that would eventually irritate much of the world. The opposition has never scared me, as long as I know I am being honest. The great thing about living in America is that the consequences for speaking openly are not incredibly dire relative to some countries around the world. There are places in which prison or execution are the prices being paid by those who challenge the government. Those who fight for justice in the face of such adversity are the real heroes in this world.

My experience with the school system was terrible, humiliating and downright depressing. My grades were usually horrible and I hated going to school. My typical report card consisted of one B (perhaps in Physical Education), 2 or 3 Cs, a D or two, and at least one F. When my report card would have two Fs, my mother usually gave me a "whoopin" for getting so many low grades. So, I tried to keep the pathetic grades to a minimum. Taking an exam at school was always a stressful experience, full of stomach aches and a type of pain that I can barely write about. Perhaps if I'd had someone to help me with my homework, the fear would not have been so intense.

My uncle was my older brother figure, the guy I sort of looked up to. But it didn't take long for me to realize that he was not someone worth looking up to and hardly a man worth respecting. I saw him going in and out of jail for only God-knows-what, creating a long streak of tears and disappointment. If I'd had a more reliable older brother figure, he would have taught me to have confidence at an early age. I am a very confident man, but I was not a confident child. An older brother or perhaps a father who'd spent more time with me could have taught me to speak to girls. Perhaps then I would have gotten a date before the age of 17. But then again, getting what you want too easily can make you spoiled.

When I was a 17-year-old Taco Bell employee, I got my first girlfriend. She was as beautiful as the sun is bright and had a body out of a magazine. Naturally, this girlfriend and I "discovered" this thing called "sex," which we practiced more than a busy attorney practices law. I then found out that there was another, less exciting side of sex called "pregnancy." That is when my daughter was born.

I had an animal attraction to the mother of my child, but our families were from "different sides of the tracks." Even though there was not a lot of education in my family, my parents did finish college when they were 30 years old. My mother barely squeaked through school with 2 kids and 2 jobs, but she made it. My father was a good student who also joined the police force near his 30th birthday. I saw my parents engage in the type of upward mobility that would have made George and Weezy proud.

They taught me that you should never be complacent with what you've got; you should always go for more.

Black upward social mobility was something I came to expect and it was something I learned directly from watching my parents. I also learned from my father, the stoic general who reminds me of Bill Cosby, to keep things simple and to always be tough. If you want to quit smoking, you just quit. You don't whine and cry over it, ask for sympathy or sit around on your ass hoping that someone will invent a patch or a pill to make you feel better. You just take the cigarette out of your mouth and don't put it back. If you want to lose weight, you don't sign up for a special diet. You don't sue McDonald's for feeding you fattening food. You take your fat, bloated ass to the gym and work out. You could say that this was an old man's version of "keeping it real" or more accurately, "keeping it real simple." I inherited this simplicity of life from my father. My PhD taught me to see the complex picture and appreciate it. But within the complexities, there are usually simplified patterns that explain the bulk of the process. That is what has allowed me to travel so easily between the 20-second sound bites of national television to the excessive, self-indulgent mental masturbation that occurs regularly in academia ("Mental masturbation" is a common term to describe those who analyze for the sake of analysis and don't actually solve real problems when doing so. Many professors are chronic mental masturbators).

Sometimes we want things to be simple, but they are not. We see people do things that don't make sense to us and we are quick to presume that they are just stupid or crazy. If a poor single mother makes peculiar purchasing or parenting decisions, we spend far less time understanding her logic than we spend condemning her choices. The

23

reality is that there are times when a second layer of analysis is necessary to understand where the other individual is coming from. Life is not always as black and white as we want to believe, there are usually shades of gray. At the same time, things are not always as complicated as we believe them to be either.

When my daughter was about to be born, I recall a powerful and distinct difference between the reaction of my family and that of my daughter's mother. In my family, getting pregnant as a teenager is no cause for celebration. It's not as if they tell you to jump off a bridge, but they aren't going to have a party. There is a discussion about the future and how you plan to create a good life for yourself with a child in tow. So, even though my grades were terrible and one counselor after another told me that I was not "college material", the pending birth of my daughter made college a necessity.

On the other side of "the tracks," the reaction to my daughter's birth was vastly different. There was celebration and complete, utter joy as if having a child at 18 was what you were *supposed* to do. After all, if you've already finished high school, what more is there to do? At that point, you're supposed to have a child, get a job, maybe get married one day and live happily ever after. Terms like "college", "graduate school" or "professional career" weren't used very much in day-to-day conversation.

My daughter being born was a bit of an awakening for me. Actually, it was like being shaken out of a bad dream and realizing that your life is even more of a nightmare than the bad dream from which you've just emerged. The fear of having a child in this society and not being able to take care of that child was incredibly overwhelming, and I wasn't quite sure what to do.

I did know (from watching others in my family and listening to my grandmother discuss how much she wished she'd gotten an education) that learning might provide a way out of my circumstances. I certainly knew that taking the $500 scholarship I had to the University of Kentucky was more promising than my other options: working for minimum wage or fighting in the war in Iraq. This Iraq War in the early 1990s was the first time the Bush family invaded another nation's sovereignty for no good reason. The second war, waged by Bush junior years later, would be equally embarrassing for the nation and incredibly damaging to the Bush family legacy.

Once I arrived on the University of Kentucky campus, I was sure I did not belong. If I couldn't make good grades in high school, there was no reason to believe that I could do so in college. After all, the students carried backpacks all the time and wore the tiny little glasses that made them look smart. White kids with tiny glasses were scary to me and I didn't think I could compete.

But I knew that I didn't want my daughter to have a deadbeat for a father, and I knew that I didn't want to get "pimped" for the rest of my life. I knew that education might be my only chance at prosperity, so I focused my mind on studying. The problem was that I didn't quite know how to study, since I'd never done it before.

Inspired by my newfound desire to excel academically, I called my mother on the phone and proudly said, "Mama, I'm gonna try to make straight A's this year."

My mother, who's always been my greatest cheerleader, realized that I might be setting myself up for failure. So, breathing a sigh of reality into the situation she simply said, "Now baby, don't get your hopes up too high." It wasn't that my mother was trying to dissuade me from shooting for the stars. She just didn't want me to miss the stars and land in the gutter. Baby-steps are typically the most productive way to move through life, and I was trying to sprint before walking. My mother had seen my report card all those years, and with all the black youth who head to college each year only to return home, it makes sense that she would be concerned that I might be setting my goals too high.

The loss of the relationship with my daughter's mother was even more disappointing. My renewed commitment to education broke down our relationship, as I am sure there are more exciting and better looking men in the world who don't spend every day with their nose in a book. Shortly after my daughter was born, her mother left to be with another man. Apparently, I'd become a bit of a drag.

But I stayed focused. I didn't know how to study, but I'd played sports. If playing sports teaches us anything, it teaches us how to work hard, how to work consistently and how to be tough. I knew that if you want to win a championship in 3 weeks, you should begin practicing right away. You don't wait until the last minute. I also knew that if you want to defeat the competition, you need to practice harder and more consistently than your opponent.

Every day, I went to the library. But I didn't tell my friends I was going to the library to study. I simply told them that I was "going to practice." I don't think they had a damn clue what I meant, but I didn't care. I was going to practice and I was going to practice hard. I was going to be the best and I was going to give 100%. High school sports taught me how to do that.

At the end of the first semester, I found out that my perceptions and expectations were pleasantly off-track. I'd gone the entire 16-and-a-half weeks of school thinking that I was barely hanging on. I thought I was the dumb guy trying to keep up with the smart kids. What I soon realized was that I was actually pushing harder and more consistently than all of my classmates. I earned a 4.0 that semester, the first time in my life that I'd ever come close to making straight As. It was the most amazing feeling I've ever had.

I still remember picking up my report card out of the mailbox, in anticipation of the fact that this could be the day where all my hard work finally paid off. After getting confirmation that my expectations were accurate, my mother's house was suddenly the location of the wildest house party you could ever imagine. I was dancing with my mother and singing with my sister and brother. I'd finally arrived at the destiny God created for me.

For me, academic achievement was the ultimate prison break. One great semester killed all the demons planted in my soul by one high school guidance counselor after another who'd sent me to special education classes. I had no idea that I was just a statistic in an overseer-like school system, in which teachers from the suburbs work to consistently destroy the futures of black children from the inner city. While most teachers work hard to do their jobs well, the reality is that many of us cannot overcome the disease of systemic racism. Black boys are 5 times more likely to be put in special education than white boys and their teachers, unable to understand their genius, are complicit in the destruction of the futures of these children.

My words are not intended to indict every teacher in America. It is to simply say that when millions of dreams are being destroyed one year after the next, there should be a national mandate to fix the problem. The War on Terror of the Bush Administration should have been replaced by a War on Educational Terrorism. Our society's conclusion that all of these children are simply choosing to destroy their futures is absolutely intolerable and would not be accepted if these were kids in the suburbs.

After my first semester in college, it was time to choose a major. I looked at the academic bulletin, which described each major and the classes necessary to complete it. I'd come to analyze, memorize and understand the bulletin as if it were my best friend. Growing up without a strong sense of trust in others led me to fully understand the importance of personal responsibility. If I'd passively allowed some college guidance counselor to send me to the wrong classes, I would only have myself to blame. Passive behavior is acceptable for children who must yield to adults, but by 18, I'd become a man.

These lessons of responsibility came from my parents. Although my father was a police officer, I was made fully aware that if I went to college and got arrested, he would not come bail me out of jail. I would not have the same benefits as my friends, whose parents would cover for them every time they screwed up. When I was 17 and a half, my father told me, "When you turn 18, you have 6 months to leave. I don't care where you go or what you do, but you've got to get the hell out of here."

When I was a freshman in college and my pockets were empty, I called my mother to ask for help. In my best puppy dog voice, I said "Mama, I don't have any money for food!" She said "Wow, that's tough. So what you going to do about that?"

That is when I learned to get a job.

I noticed the importance of these lessons later in life, as I saw many of my 30-year-old friends living at home and living off their parents like teenagers. I'd learned to support myself from the age of 18. During college, although I had almost no financial support from my parents, I usually had more money than most of my friends. I'd learned the value of time management and working two jobs, which put a lot more money in my pocket than I would have gotten by bumming from my parents.

All through college, I never engaged in the massive alcohol consumption that now plagues our campuses. It wasn't because I was an angel; I was actually the class clown. I didn't drink because it simply didn't make sense to me: I noticed that binge drinking made your breath stink, led you to do things you might regret and put your well-being at risk. I was a painfully shy nerd with low self-esteem, but even I was strong enough to back away from really stupid behavior.

By embracing my own personal power, I was able to obtain the benefits of financial freedom very early in life, and I haven't looked back since. This was my first taste of what money means to all of us. Money is not an ends in itself, but a means to a better life. This is not only true for the individual, but for the collective as well. Money, as a tool for life enhancement, can lead to a rich and meaningful existence full of purpose, liberation and tremendous well-being.

On the other hand, a lack of financial resources can lead to the opposite effect: a challenging and unfulfilled life, full of unsavory activities pursued solely to obtain the resources necessary to survive. As long as you are not financially independent, you are not liberated, because the person who controls your access to critical resources ultimately controls your access to psychological freedom. The easiest way to control a man's soul is to know that you are the reason that his children are able to eat. Few men or women are empowered enough to challenge those who control their purse strings. Education was my first opportunity to understand this valuable lesson.

When asked to pick a college major, I chose Finance. I chose Finance as my major for one reason: I'd known what it was like to be broke, and I now wanted to see what it was like to have money. My parents always put food on the table, and I can remember the struggles. But my father and mother also worked hard through the years to obtain upward mobility, and desperately wanted their children to have a better life. I was determined to make that happen for my own child as well.

I only knew one thing about my new major, Finance: it was all about money. I figured that if I learned money and studied money someone would pay me money to talk about money.   These words certainly rang true, and at the age of 18, I began my long journey toward academic and personal discovery.

I took this diversion into my personal and academic background to help you get a sense of who I am. I am a believer that understanding the roots of a man helps to interpret the leaves that fall from his intellectual tree. I can literally point to the age of 18 as a turning point in my life, the time when I could have easily taken a right or left turn. I could have easily become the man washing your car wondering if I could have ever been a college professor. Of course I would have then realized that being a professor, let alone one giving commentary on CNN, was just an unrealistic pipe dream meant for someone else.

Chapter 4

Nicky Barnes and Frank Lucas, "The American Gangster"

I recently watched two movies about major drug kingpins during the 1970s, Nicky Barnes and Frank Lucas. Both of them made a lot of money, both of them dealt drugs in Harlem, both of them went to prison and took many of their friends and associates down with them. Each man earned over 2 million dollars per week on a regular basis, which will surely be considered a great deal of money even 80 years from today.

I learn from watching epic dramas from the past, because you can see a man or woman's rise and fall with a perspective they never had. The main characters of the story don't have the power of foresight and hindsight at the same time to know when their reign is going to end. They don't know if they are at the bottom of the mountain or at the peak of it.

Many people of color had a strange admiration for both Barnes and Lucas. Even I was one of those people (to a point), as I listened proudly while someone explained how Frank Lucas was the first major Harlem drug dealer to circumvent the mafia and find his own distribution channels. The far flashier Nicky Barnes was incredibly effective as well, controlling major Harlem real estate in the drug trade.

Without placing moral judgment on the decision to sell drugs (which I certainly do not condone), we can use the experiences of Barnes and Lucas to teach us a couple of lessons about finance, investing and life. First, there is a consistent tradeoff between risk and return. In finance, as in life, those who take the most risk experience the most volatility. If the risks are carefully calculated, the risky investors also experience the greatest return on their investments. Barnes and Lucas did not make money because no one else wanted it or because no one else had the skill to do what they did. A large portion of their returns were earned because they were the only ones willing to engage in the lifestyle of a drug dealer and to take the risks necessary to rise to the top of the drug ladder.

If you'll notice, the drug king pin is usually one of the strongest members of the organization. He/she is mentally strong and sometimes even physically strong. He is willing to do things other human beings, even those in the same industry, are unwilling to do. There is a scene in "American Gangster" in which Frank Lucas sees his rival on the street, casually approaches him, and shoots him in the head in broad daylight. He then walks back to his favorite restaurant and finishes eating breakfast. While Hollywood most likely romanticized actual events a bit, situations like this are part of the risk/return tradeoff Lucas made to establish his dominance in the industry.

When Lucas was willing to fly all the way to Vietnam to develop direct connections with drug suppliers in the poppy fields, this was also part of the risk he endured that led him to have a much greater return than his rivals. He could just as easily have settled down as a regular drug runner and taken the payments that came with such activity.

The bulk of the risk/return tradeoff was witnessed by Barnes' and Lucas' choice to enter into the lifestyle of a drug dealer in the first place. But risk has a downside, as both men watched their personal stories end badly. Lucas got many members of his own family killed or sent to prison. Barnes sent many of his associates to prison and is known to this day as one of the most infamous "snitches" in the history of New York City. Their periods of power were short-lived, but their lives were long enough for them to have tremendous regret for what they'd done to others.

One can argue that being impoverished black men in America made it easier for Barnes and Lucas to take these risks. Had they been middle class suburban kids receiving good educations, I conjecture that neither Lucas nor Barnes would have ended up on the street selling drugs. Both of them were considered incredibly intelligent by their peers and probably had the intellect to attend Harvard Medical School. But the circumstances that surround a man can play a strong role in his incentive to take risk. Risk is no longer risky when the individual has very little to lose.

You can compare risk-taking to playing a video game. In a video game, your character can die, but you are not worried. You're not worried because dying only means you must restart the game. Therefore, you may be willing to take chances when playing a video game that you would not take in real life. Your perception of risk changes based upon your incentives and consequences for taking on the risk. Secondly, if you are an individual with nothing to lose, the same risk will be perceived differently by yourself than it would be by others. Middle class African-Americans have a great deal to lose, which is why most of us do not take many social or political risks. My goal is to talk about how we can "reduce the weight" of taking risks, so that we are not only more empowered to assume risk, we are in a better position to take risks in the first place. Achieving financial security reduces the consequences of taking political and social risks.

Another lesson from the experience of Barnes and Lucas was the secondary message of black liberation. Many in the black community, for various reasons, came to see Barnes and Lucas as models of inspiration. In the Barnes documentary, a child was asked if New York Yankees baseball star Reggie Jackson was his hero after hitting three homeruns in the World Series the night before. He said that his hero was not Jackson, but Nicky Barnes.

Barnes' and Lucas' financial prosperity was seen as a path to get away from the punitive grip of white America, and to release the firm grip that racism has historically had on the necks of African-Americans. Lucas was a source of pride to some because he became the boss and didn't appear to have to answer to anyone. It was hard to believe that a black man could achieve such autonomy, so racial ignorance actually kept Lucas under the radar for quite a while. Most of the FBI agents and other criminals felt it impossible that a black man could be running his own operation. Barnes was considered a man who gave back to the community on some level, and for that he received respect and admiration. The fact that he was giving back to the community while simultaneously hooking many members of the community on drugs was an awkward reality, but it was accepted. The drug addicts were considered the weakest members of society, and the notion of preying on the weak to enhance the coffers of the strong was not considered such a bad thing. I cannot say that I agree with this assessment, since I am in favor of supporting and protecting the weak, while helping all of us to learn to be strong.

An addendum to the legacies of Barnes and Lucas should be the US. Government's bogus War on Drugs. Ronald Reagan, by far one of the most damaging presidents in American history, created the war on drugs to allegedly get drugs off the street, but this commitment was far from sincere. While creating strong drug laws that led to the incarcerations of tens of thousands of black men, he simultaneously allowed South American drug Lords to flood drugs into the black community without fear of prosecution. One of Nicky Barnes' associates said it best when he mentioned that the biggest criminals in America are typically the ones at the top of the social ladder. Given his connections to the failed War on Drugs and South American drug cartels, it appears that Ronald Reagan was associated with many of the greatest criminals in American history.

The most tragic part of the story of Barnes and Lucas was that their quest for money led them to neglect their most valuable assets: family, friends, freedom and mental health. The pursuit of additional revenue led to tremendous pain for those they loved, and ultimately led to the loss of the very freedom they'd worked so hard to obtain. But their story is not uncommon for drug dealers in America, as it shows that in spite of the high rewards received for taking risk, the risk itself may not be calculated, intelligent or rational.

An additional lesson from the sagas of Lucas and Barnes is that of wealth building. Both men and their colleagues earned huge sums of money. My question as a financial expert was to ask, "What did they do with this money? How did they manage it? What was their exit strategy?" I would argue that sound investing throughout the process could have created a window for these men to leave their industries without being touched by the federal government. The same is true for Ricky Ross, another powerful drug kingpin in Los Angeles. Ross, also a highly intelligent man, left the drug game but ran out of money soon afterward. An individual earning over two-million dollars per week should never run out of money if that money is being managed correctly.

I am going to stop judging the drug dealers for a second and put them in the same category as the rest of the pharmaceutical sales companies across America. Everyone in this group, relatively speaking, has the same purpose: to provide medication for people to help them move beyond their problems. An addiction to heroine is probably more difficult to achieve than an addiction to Oxycontin, because the drug is less readily available. Also, pure financial theory allows for limited digressions from morality to help us to explore the analytical side of an issue.

All of the drug dealers I've mentioned possessed tremendous intelligence, high incomes, a great deal of ambition, and a lot of courage. Their primary mistake, like many of us in black America, is not that they didn't have a high enough income. It was that this income was not being translated into *wealth*. You can think of income as water coming out of a faucet. The water quenches your immediate thirst and helps you get through the day. No matter how healthy you are, several days without liquidity will lead to certain death.

The same is true for business. Many profitable businesses fail every year because they don't have access to the liquidity they need to continue operations. An illiquid firm, although it has many clients who owe it money, can't pay the bills and is forced into bankruptcy.

That is why the term "liquidity" is an excellent descriptor of cash-based income.

The problem with the income and liquidity that flows out of our financial faucets is that when the faucet is turned off, we die of financial thirst. Many people with high incomes could not keep their homes for another 2 months if they were to lose their jobs. That's because they've come to rely on the source of liquidity as their avenue for sustenance and survival. The same is true of Barnes, Lucas and Ross, the men I describe above. They were thirsty men who kept going to the same well of drug dealing, rather than building a well of their own.

Now, imagine someone taking the water that comes out of the faucet, drinking some of it, and putting the rest into a container. Then, imagine that the person takes the container and puts it in the freezer. The freezer may have a tiny leak at the top that continuously drops water onto the block of ice he has created, allowing the block of ice to grow on its own. In time, if the faucet stops producing, this individual can then melt off pieces of ice into water and have a drink anytime he wants.

The analogy above describes the difference between wealth building and having a high income. He who drinks from the biggest faucet has the greatest opportunity to quench his thirst and perhaps the thirst of others. But even those with big faucets can become slaves to the source of their liquidity. Those who freeze some of their water and form a block of ice for the freezer are slowly liberating themselves from dependence on their previous source of income. They are building CAPITAL. The water leaking from the freezer and dropping onto the block of ice is the interest being earned on your investments. Money has a magical way of growing astronomically in a relatively short amount of time when one is a long-term investor. This additional liquidity dropping on top of the ice, in addition to the ice being placed in the freezer every day, creates the large block of liquid which comes to form the foundation of wealth ultimately possessed by the individual.

I don't judge Barnes, Lucas or Ross for choosing to become drug dealers. I am not able, for one second, to say that I would not have considered an illegal trade myself under certain circumstances. Those of us who say we would never commit illegal acts under any circumstances are probably being delusional. The structural challenges of our operating environment can have a strong influence on our personal incentives. Each of these men, when interviewed, discussed the trauma of poverty and watching their mothers struggle. We all have different reactions to such discomfort.

Additionally, after witnessing the criminal activity of the Bush administration, the immoral behavior of pharmaceutical companies, and the criminal behavior of those who destroyed our financial system, I do not feel compelled to judge drug dealers any more harshly than I judge the rest of our business and political leadership. Where I fault Barnes, Lucas and Ross is that, in all their intelligence, power and creativity, they did not appear to focus on wealth building so they could eventually remove themselves from the huge risks they were imposing on themselves and their families. I also hold them accountable for their role in the destruction of the black community via drug dealing. So, I can't let them off the hook completely.

When an individual has nothing to lose, he is like a player in a basketball game in which he is 30 points behind. To have a chance to win, you have to take a lot of 3 point shots, run a strong defensive press, and engage in a series of risky strategies to get yourself back in the game. But once you've gotten into the game and taken a comfortable lead, it is critical that you begin the process of risk reduction and minimization. Many drug dealers understand this concept on some level, because the highest ranking members of the organization are usually the ones who never touch the drugs and rarely discuss them. They insulate themselves from the risks of the industry. This same logic should be applied to financial management; it doesn't just apply to drug dealers. Any person who takes risk to acquire wealth should then engage in the process of reducing their risks in order to protect and preserve the wealth they've accumulated. Barnes and Lucas did not effectively manage risk, and many middle and upper class African Americans do not protect their wealth either.

Chapter 5

Finance 101: The Structure of the Money Game in America

When I teach introductory finance courses to college students, we start with the foundation of capitalism. I don't always agree with everything taught in Financial Theory, but professors don't have much of a choice. I am obligated to ensure that my students learn the foundations of our discipline, no matter how peculiar those theoretical foundations may be. At that point, I am given some academic liberty to discuss potential flaws in the theory or alternative interpretations. Such analysis is critical, given that African-Americans were not invited to the table when the foundations of financial theory and capitalism were created. Therefore, to ensure that we are not simply eating food prepared by someone else, we must ultimately manage and utilize altered tools of thought so that they can be productively employed for the advancement of the black community.

My ultimate goal is not to think for the students, it is to teach them to think for themselves. When teaching Capitalism 101, the first place we start is with the firm: why the firm exists, the incentives of the firm, and how firms succeed. In capitalism, the purpose of the firm and its management is to do one thing: Maximize shareholder wealth. The core of financial theory says very little about doing what is morally right. It says almost nothing about taking care of the environment. It says very little about paying workers a decent wage, keeping jobs in the US, or giving a damn about people. It says that your sole and primary obligation is to protect and support the interests of the individuals who control the firm. The controllers of the firm are, for the most part, the individuals who supply the capital. In most cases, they might be called shareholders. So, if the shareholders were stars in the NFL, the firm managers would be their agents. The agent (manager) has a fiduciary responsibility to protect the interests of the principal (shareholder) at all costs.

Tangential issues, such as treating suppliers fairly, taking care of your workers, or protecting the environment eventually become part of the capitalist conversation, but only on a secondary level. According to financial theory, you only manage these social externalities to the extent that they help you achieve your primary objective: Maximizing shareholder wealth. In other words, making money is the game, and everything else is just a half time show.

Let's consider an example. If a profitable firm is deciding what to do with its toxic waste, the managers of that firm are surely going to check the law to determine what options they have. They are not typically looking to do "the right thing", but rather, "doing the right thing" becomes synonymous with "doing the legal thing" or "doing the profitable thing". Managers realize that breaking the law is not going to further their interest in maximizing shareholder wealth, so they will work within the law to dispose their waste as cost effectively as possible.

But even violating the law becomes an option if the price of the violation constitutes a sound financial investment. Assume it costs a company $100 million dollars per year to dispose of toxic waste, but they realize that illegally disposing of the waste will cost them $5 million per year in fines. Many companies then have a direct financial incentive to illegally dispose of the waste and endure the associated fines.

I recall giving a speech at a university in Upstate New York. We were talking about wealth building for the black community and how black folks can remove themselves from the underbelly of American capitalism. I'd heard this school had a reputation for strong liberalism and I was looking forward to addressing the audience. A young white female in the back of the room raised her hand to ask me a question. She said "How can you support a system that enslaves people?"

The woman was clearly offended by my mere presence as a financial expert and apparent supporter of capitalism. I could immediately tell that, no matter what my answer was, she was going to hate me and wish death upon my children. She didn't realize that I am not just a Finance Professor, but also a closet socialist in many contexts. While I am not one who wants to live in a socialist society, I do understand that capitalism and socialism must balance one another in any society that alleges to embrace human compassion.

I answered the student as best I could. But honestly, it seemed that I wouldn't be able to say much of anything to change her mind. College students, as impressionable as they are, can sometimes become very black and white and idealistically pure in their viewpoints. Idealism is a wonderful thing, but if one is not careful, it can lead to blind self-righteousness. Few things in life are 100% bad or good, and a true understanding of any concept requires the individual to analyze the shades of gray that lie in between.

While I am a fan of capitalism as a source of human motivation, I've never been a fan of "Capitalism gone wild". In addition to seeing the benefits of capitalism, I've also studied the dirty side. The Ford Motor Company issued a memo in the 1970s in which they acknowledged that a certain number of their cars were going to explode each year, due to a technical malfunction in the production of the Pinto. After calculating the cost of the explosions and subsequent lawsuits, they decided not to recall the unsafe vehicles. In other words, they were willing to incur the financial cost of lawsuits from families of the dead and injured rather than actually spend the money necessary to recall the cars.

The health care industry is another example. While US citizens pay more in health care costs than any other country in the world, the quality of care is mediocre at best. Corporations are trained to put a price on human life, so an individual without the insurance necessary to obtain life saving surgery is simply left to die. The Hippocratic Oath taken by doctors easily becomes the hypocritical oath, as doctors who've promised to save lives are indirectly forced to allow their low-income patients to visit the Grim Reaper.

The profit motive clearly comes into play for pharmaceutical companies, who are now allowed to advertise their drugs in order to find creative ways to get consumers to use their products. The pressure from shareholders to continue to achieve growth in profits and revenues pushes the industry over the top to do whatever it can to feed the insatiable monster of profit maximization and growth. We no longer need corner drug dealers, as the pharmaceutical companies have gladly replaced the thrill of illegal drugs.

This monster of profitability can be frightening as it feeds upon itself year after year. No matter how strong or profitable a company is, there is always pressure to surpass the prior year's performance. Stocks are valued based on growth expectations, and earning the same amount in profits one year after another will surely get the CEO fired. While one might be tempted to blame firm managers for perpetuating this system of profit maximization and the social norms that come along with it, the reality is that managers have little power over the system, since bad managers simply get replaced. The new guy is always willing to do what the old guy would not, so blaming CEOs for capitalist problems is like blaming rappers for negative hip hop. Rather than expecting individuals within a system to suddenly commit to doing the right thing, it can sometimes be more effective to challenge the system itself.

Hip hop, often the subject of tremendous criticism, is a perfect example of capitalism gone wild. Oprah Winfrey is one of the 10 people I respect the most on this planet. However, she is not beyond being critiqued.

Her Town Hall Meeting on hip hop in 2007 was, to me, flawed and unnecessarily limited in scope. In response to the objectionable imagery presented in commercialized hip hop, Winfrey decided to address the issue. The guests on the show included many critics of hip hop, and a couple of very "safe" rappers, not the "gangster rappers" Winfrey was most upset about. I wasn't quite sure how Oprah expected to have a critical dialogue about a topic without having a guest willing to firmly and intelligently represent the opposing point of view. It was my speculation, based on comments Winfrey has made about rappers in the past, that she was hesitant to even provide a platform to individuals she considers to be menaces to society.

For example, the rapper Ice Cube has never been invited on The Oprah Winfrey Show, although she has featured some of his family films.

Additionally, the rapper Ludacris was on the show, chastised in public and had his responses to Oprah edited out of the final tape that aired in front of the nation. On some CNN appearances and another appearance with Shock Jock Diva Wendy Williams, I made it clear that I did not agree with Oprah's approach to this complex issue.

Many critics of hip hop are as misguided as the teenagers who listen to the music when it comes to choosing a target for their disdain. The artist is clearly the most visible part of the process, and one can easily interpret the artist to be the power broker, as well as the final stopping point for the buck of responsibility. The artist, as the individual who spits out the lyrics we find so repulsive, seems to clearly be the one who can make the bad lyrics stop.

The idea that the artist can make all the problems of hip hop go away is certainly true in one sense: If the rapper stops rapping, then the rapping will stop. The problem is that the rapper himself is also a cog in the broad wheel of capitalism. He/she is nothing more than a pawn on a great corporate battlefield that has a long list of rappers ready to take his position as soon as he leaves the airwaves.

Most artists I've met, even the most powerful ones, don't have the ability to change the nature of their lyrics without the permission of a higher corporate power. Ludacris, the artist Oprah reluctantly brought onto her show and proceeded to treat quite rudely, can certainly change the nature of his music to suit Oprah's expectations. He could even sell records in that context. He would not be likely to sell as many records as he did before, but he could certainly earn a nice return on the investment of his corporate parent.

The problem with the alternative approach Ludacris could take in my example is that everything is relative in the eyes of the corporate monster. If you sold a million records with your last album release, then anything less than that is going to be considered a failure. Oprah should understand this tradeoff as much as anyone. If her show has 4 million viewers per day and the studio expects 6 million, she is considered a disappointment. She is expected to give the soccer moms *exactly* what they want in order for the company to maximize shareholder wealth. The rapper Ludacris, with his newfound consciousness, may release music that makes Oprah and others feel comfortable, only to find that the corporate monster is already seeking out his replacement. The machine survives, and rogue individuals typically do not.

There is also a clear divergence in risk tolerance between the artist at the record label and the corporate manager, thus leading to another serious conflict of interest. Corporations are not trying to get rich; they are trying to STAY rich and GET RICHER. When one is trying to get rich, like the broke artist who doesn't have a nickel to his name, he is willing to take chances in order to find fortune. Also, the very virtue of artistic expression dictates that the artist must take certain risks in order to have his or her work noticed by others.

Corporations, when trying to stay rich and get richer, do all they can to avoid taking risk. Any risk endured is carefully calculated risk that will surely lead to higher profitability within the constraints of capital preservation. So, when the head of a major record label is having a conversation with his artist, the conversation might go something like this:

Artist (the rapper "Cash Money"): I have this great idea for something that is going to be even better than "Booties, Hoes and Beyatches" my last album. It's also going to be more positive for the black community. I am going to call it "Books, Homework and Better Grades".

Mr. Executive: Wow Cash Money, that's a great idea. But "Booties, Hoes and Beyatches" did incredibly well last year, and we were thinking that you could release "More Booties, Extra Hoes and Too Many Beyatches". Now that would be hot and just freakin jiggy!

Artist: Yea, well Oprah said that this kind of music is bad for the community, and I did graduate from college. So, I know the value of making good grades in school. I want to provide inspiration for black people and do something good with my life.

Mr. Executive: That's nice Cash Money, and I "feel you dawg," really I do. The problem is that black people aren't the ones buying your records. Our survey data shows that white kids from the suburbs are buying your music, and they see you as the guy who gets it "poppin" (holding two fingers in the air, resembling quotations) in the club.

Our projections say that this new idea of yours probably won't sell nearly as well as your last album, so we've got a problem. We gave you your big break and kinda need you to stay focused here. I know you want to save the world, but if you make a style of music that causes you to lose your fan base, there is always going to be another kid from the projects willing to take your spot. So, not only are you not going to make a difference, you are also going to lose your deal, your fame, your money, your bling, your house, your fine-ass women, and all the other things that are near and dear to you.

Artist: Ah-ight man. You right. I'll get to the studio.

Hip hop, in its purest form, is not problematic. It is a powerful, broad social movement with thousands of forms of expression. It reflects the best of black genius and creativity and has stretched its power across the world. But prominent commercialized hip hop becomes a marriage between artistic expression and the corporate monster. Like any other form of creative performance, the corporate monster's commitment to the bottom line ultimately dilutes the initial purpose of the art form. This is no different from what happens in Hollywood, as every talented actor consistently wonders why Sylvester Stallone has been featured in so many films.

The awkward, deformed nature of commercialized hip hop relates to the continued promotion and distribution of the most embarrassing and vile forms of expression. These forms have as much a right to exist as any other, but the continuous focus on negative brands of hip hop, those which lead to counter-productive cultural outcomes is disturbing to almost anyone. What's most interesting is that these messages are not being created nor distributed to appeal to African-Americans, since we are not the ones who purchase the music. They are distributed by white corporations for a predominantly white audience, with the black community sitting as a silent partner in the consumption and distribution process.

The distribution of negative hip hop is like one person throwing a cigarette across the room to another, with a child standing beneath the path of the cigarette, being sprinkled and burned with ashes. Corporate America is the group passing the cigarette, white youth are the ones catching the cigarette and black youth represent the child being burned by ashes as the cigarette hovers above. Singular media representations of African-Americans lead black youth to see entertainers as role models. Black youth proceed to imitate the behavior of the individuals they see on TV. White youth, on the other hand, have a variety of white images to embrace on the airwaves. Therefore, they are not constrained by the image of the rapper or basketball player as their dominant role model.

There are many forms of hip hop that are incredibly productive and entertaining. Many of these forms might actually sell if they were given a chance. The problem is that the corporate monster is not interested in risking capital to find out what "might" sell. It is only willing to invest capital in things that "will" sell. The monster's intolerance for unnecessary risk does not compel it to consider alternative forms of hip hop music when a proven product is already available. Also, the corporate monster has no concern for any negative side effects produced by the music, especially if those effects do not occur in the communities of those who provide the capital. Therefore, there is no incentive to be socially responsible in music distribution, since this is like making a chemical product and dumping the waste in someone else's neighborhood.

Recall, Finance 101 teaches that you are only socially responsible to the extent that it impacts your bottom line. So, even if record labels were run by African-Americans (consider BET and Bob Johnson, discussed later in the book, as a prime example), the corporate monster is trained to only respond to issues of social responsibility to the extent that there is a financial or legal backlash for irresponsible actions. BET, even when it was run by

African-Americans, did not feel enough of a backlash from the black community to justify changing its programming format. So, to this end, Oprah Winfrey and Bill Cosby are right that part of the responsibility for correcting problematic corporate behavior is to hold the consumer accountable for what he/she is willing to accept.

Kane West is a highly successful artist who forced his way into hip hop after being told that rapping about Jesus and education was not going to work. What is also interesting about the Kanye West model is that his experience serves as a lesson regarding what steps we can take as a community to improve the state of hip hop for the long-term. The difference between West and other artists is that West did not wait for a label to sign him. Waiting would have destroyed his career, since no major record label was willing to risk its capital on a type of hip hop that was not proven to be maximally profitable. Even gangster rap was not capitalized until it was proven to be successful. Instead, West obtained his own capital and invested in the creation of his own music video.

Kanye and his mother, Dr. Donda West, not only saw hip hop as a form of political expression, they had enough understanding of the commercialization process to get Kanye's career started. The same could be true for other artists who can appreciate the double bottom line of social consciousness, meshed with their desire for creative expression.

The talented rapper Method Man made a song in the 90s with the chorus, "Cream (money) moves everything around me." If money moves everything around you, you're in trouble.

Any corporate agent who focuses solely on the one-dimensional bottom line may obtain a tremendous amount of money, all at the expense of their most valuable social and moral assets. Additionally, capital accumulation is critical to being able to commit to the double bottom line of the black community, as it is nonsensical to expect predominantly white corporations to risk their financial capital to support African-American social norms. America is a racist society, and when it comes to things Americans care about, the black community is not very high on the list.

To summarize, every rapper in America should go to business school for at least a little while. They should realize that the corporate monster creates two things: Pimps and hoes. I don't use the term "hoe" in a gender-based way; I used it to refer to the individual who does not control his or her own destiny. Both pimps and hoes can be either male or female. The pimps are those who have the capital and control the capital. The hoes are those who are subject to the whims of those who control the capital. Rappers are not pimps, most of them are hoes.

What is also true is that many of us make ourselves into "high priced hoes" by committing to the needs of the corporate monster without a long-term plan for accumulating the capital that will allow us to control our own destiny. Many of my friends who are professors, doctors and lawyers are the first to assume that hip hop artists are ignorant. All the while, my professional friends have also chosen to make themselves slaves of the corporate monster. They become shackled by excessive debt, high car notes and an addiction to a high salary as they become continuously codependent upon the financial faucet feeding them their critical liquidity. Eventually, they find themselves socially castrated, and highly ineffective: Well-trained black academics sat and quietly watched African-Americans die during Hurricane Katrina, doctors watch patients die because they don't have insurance, and attorneys sit idly by as black men go to prison by the boatload without adequate representation.

Truth be told, many of us are controlled and manipulated by our environments. I would like to see us, as people of color, have the option of controlling the processes which sustain us. But the idea of being in control of the corporate monster does not necessarily imply that we focus solely on the traditional objective of profit maximization. As I mentioned earlier, unfettered capitalism ultimately destroys a society: The underclass becomes poorer and larger, and the most powerful become richer and smaller in number. Ultimately, when the poor have nothing to lose, society crumbles as most members of that society no longer have an incentive to support that society.

So, the truth is that capitalism, in its purest form, is deadly. Even in a capitalist society, some element of socialism is necessary to leave room for human compassion. The impact on the environment, children, the elderly and workers matters. So those who grab the reigns of the corporate monster can be profitable without becoming tyrants. If black people gain control of corporate America and simply repeat the actions of those before them, then we've completely lost the game.

Chapter 6

The State of the black Union and other Peculiar Venues

There is an inner circle among black public figures, and to some extent, a competition. Because the mainstream media does not allow for a diversity of black images, there are those who compete for the few slots available. This is unfortunate, but true. If the mainsteam media doesn't feel that you fit into the "black box", you are typically going to be overlooked. In the eyes of media, black public figures can be either Al Sharpton or Flavor Flav, and nothing in between.

Although I have been trained as a financial expert, TV networks typically only call on me when they want to talk about "black stuff." Surprisingly, it was Fox News, the network I have decided to ban from my appearance list, who wanted me to speak on issues that were not related to race. My decision to boycott Fox News was driven, in large part, by the disappointment I'd felt toward host Bill O'Reilly. I consider Bill O'Reilly, Sean Hannity and others like them to be not only un-American, but downright detrimental to the advancement of our great nation.

In the inner circle of black public figures, there is a hierarchy. There is, of course, Jesse Jackson and Al Sharpton at the top of the pile of black leadership. Some of this is driven by the fact that they are veterans in the fight for civil rights, far more seasoned than the rest of us. Part of their power is driven by publicity and marketing. Without the mainstream media, it would be quite challenging for anyone to get their message out to the masses, and it is incredibly disturbing that the message transmitted from one African-American to another must be processed through channels controlled by those who dislike black people. As my friend Dr. Julia Hare so eloquently explained, there is a big difference between "black leaders" and "leading blacks".

A black leader is someone who leads black people with the vigor and integrity necessary to take our people to the next level. I would put Jesse Jackson, Al Sharpton and Louis Farrakhan in that circle of leaders who've obtained strong grass roots respect from the people. Farrakhan is controversial, but respected, strong and independent.

A shining example of a "leading black" would be the Rev. Jesse Lee Peterson, one of the most ignorant black people I've ever seen on a TV screen. Rev. Peterson is the one chosen by Fox News and Sean Hannity whenever they want to find an African-American willing to make any ridiculous assertion against his own people. In my opinion, Jesse Lee Peterson is proof that you can take any silly man off the street, clean him up and make him into a TV star. Also included in this group might be Juan Williams, the man I referred to on CNN as "The eternal happy negro." Juan, in my opinion, compromised a great deal of his journalistic integrity to pursue a second career with Fox News as a black bashing poster boy for everything that is wrong with black America. I have little respect for such individuals, for they cross the line between tough love and flat out treason.

Even above Jesse Jackson and Al Sharpton on the hierarchy of black leadership are individuals like Barack Obama, who obtained his power using the same channels as many superstar hip hop artists: cross-over appeal. Obama is loved by blacks but loved more by whites. He was the shining star of America during the election, and one of the great leaders of the 20th century....or so the headlines might read.

Below Barack Obama (Level 1) and Jesse Jackson/Al Sharpton/Louis Farrakhan (Level 2), you have the scholars and other public figures. I would include Cornel West, Michael Eric Dyson and Tavis Smiley in this tier. These are individuals who are well-known in the community and the first that the media call when they want to talk about "black stuff". I do not consider myself to be part of this tier, since I am part of the young leader tier, along with Marc Lamont Hill from Temple University and Melissa Harris-Lacewell of Princeton University. Other public figures in the young leaders' tier might be Roland Martin from CNN or Eddie Glaude at Princeton. I respect all of these individuals a great deal.

All of us "black public intellectuals" know one another and bump into each other at conferences, on TV shows, and on the radio. We keep up with each other's achievements, and there is even some degree of jealousy obvious as we politely ask each other, "So how did you get on the BET Awards Show anyway?" Personally, I learned long ago that jealousy is a counter-productive emotion and you are better off working together than working apart. The problem is that white America's focus on a one dimensional portrayal of blackness does not make room for more than one "HNIC" (Head Negro in Charge). Hence, you have a pile of crabs in a barrel, all fighting for their little bit of sun.

Barack Obama, just three years before the 2008 presidential election, wasn't even on the 4th tier of this list. He barely existed, people didn't know his name. I recall someone telling me, in 2005, about some guy named "Blabbady-Blah" in Illinois, a guy that people were getting excited about. I thought "that's nice," but I don't usually keep up with local elections. Even congressmen, mayors and senators get relatively little national press, so most people don't know their names.

But Obama emerged, and he did an amazing job. Entering the presidential race during the spring of 2007, Obama stepped on a lot of toes. By refusing to kiss the pinky rings of certain black public figures, Obama was throwing a great big, "I don't give a damn" into the face of existing black leadership. No one knew him, and he was not even a regular at the State of the black Union Conference, held each year by Tavis Smiley. The idea that this relatively unknown black man was going to try to run for president and simultaneously expect overwhelming black support was considered by many to be ridiculous.

But run he did. Not only did Obama run for the white House, he had the audacity to announce his candidacy during the State of the black Union Event. While this might seem to be a relatively harmless and insignificant act, one must put it into context. "Negro airtime" is a valuable and rare commodity, and he who controls access to the media has historically been endowed with tremendous power. A multitude of black leaders all across America were lining up for a chance to appear at The State of the black Union Conference because Tavis Smiley had become the "socio-political pusher" with "the connect". He had the product, and we were all dope fiends trying to get a taste.

For Obama to go outside Tavis Smiley as his supplier of power was a huge slap in the face. Tavis Smiley is a man with tremendous talent and ambition. He is also a man who, through his actions, communicates a desire to obtain diplomatic status within the black community. He wants to be the preacher, teacher and political leader of the community. He wants to be the individual through which the message of black empowerment will and must be transferred. His access to media, as one of the premier black journalists in America, made him the ultimate go-to guy for reaching black America. This was his power, this was his beast.

More interesting was the deep relationship Smiley has with Senator Hillary Clinton. Smiley writes about the Clintons fondly in his memoirs, which were written at a time during which the Clinton family was quite popular in the black community. Bill and Hillary had even accepted Bill's inaccurate label as the "First black President". This statement was an incredible insult to the black community, since it implied that America would not even allow a black man to become the first black President. As in most notable professions, only a white man was considered qualified for the job.

Obama impressed the nation with the powerful campaign he ran against Senator Clinton. His creative use of the internet and the youth vote allowed him to use a relatively boring motto based on "hope" to capture the nation's energy and channel its frustration. He went from being an also-ran to becoming the front-runner in the election, destroying everything and everyone in his path.

Obama's greatest power came through MONEY. It was once he showed he could raise money on equal footing with Senator Clinton that African-Americans began to believe Obama had a chance. Once he won the Iowa Primary and proved that enough white people liked him, this gave black people "permission" to support him (since many were supporting Clinton in order to avoid "wasting" their vote). Money made the difference and it was the intelligent and creative application of money that put Obama over the top.

All the while, Tavis Smiley saw his stock dropping. Had Obama chosen to simply accept his role as an also-ran, Senator Clinton's rise to the white House would be Tavis' ticket to power. Senator Clinton used Tavis as one of her key gateways to the black community, as had Wal-Mart and other corporate sponsors. Tavis enjoyed being the gateway and when he saw Senator Clinton in trouble, he stepped in to support her by working to undercut the Barack Obama halo that had developed in the black community.

I am not here to say that support for Hillary was the sole reason for Smiley's disdain toward Senator Obama, but I honestly believe it played a role in the process. Part of the goal in the power game is remaining relevant. Relevance implies that you control access to something that others need, and that they can only get it through you. By surpassing Hillary Clinton in the democratic nomination process, Senator Obama was undermining Tavis Smiley's relevance as the only path for high powered white politicians to reach the black community. To use airline terminology, Tavis was the hub, but Barack Obama had become the direct flight.

Tavis' work in the community is important. But there is a difference between being an intelligent guide to enlightenment and being downright self-righteous. Tavis has a way of putting political leaders "on blast" for not showing up at his forums. When he held a debate for the Republicans in the 2008 Presidential Primaries, there were several Republican presidential candidates who chose not to attend. I understand why Tavis was upset about this, because the Republican Party is known for its racism and ignorance to the needs of the black community. Smiley responded to the Republican snub by putting the name of the candidate on the podium even if they were not appearing at the forum. This was a clear reminder to those in the audience that the leader "doesn't care about issues in the black community."

When holding the State of the black Union (some confuse it with the State of black America, a document issued each year by the Urban League), Smiley again invited as many political leaders as he could find, with Hillary Clinton being his star for the day. Senator Obama, in the middle of a heated battle for Democratic delegates in Texas and Ohio, said that he could not attend the forum. Instead, he offered his wife Michelle to attend in his place. That's when the drama got heated.

Tavis, appearing to be offended by Obama's slight toward his conference, proceeded to nibble away at Obama's heels every morning on The Tom Joyner Morning Show. The segments started with "he-say, she-say", in which Tavis claimed that no one from the Obama camp offered Michelle up for attendance. But even if they had, Tavis claimed that no spouse of a presidential candidate would be acceptable for the conference, even Bill Clinton.

I felt that Tavis' statement was misleading. It was also a slap in the face of black women everywhere who have tremendous respect for Michelle Obama. Smiley's words about the Obamas bordered on petty and angered the millions of African-Americans who'd come to believe that Barack Obama could walk on water. While I never felt that Obama could walk on water, I certainly did not understand Smiley's confused obsession with Barack Obama's behavior. Smiley's comments toward the black presidential candidate reminded me of the same double standard I can sometimes experience as a black professor. You may have black students who feel a certain degree of comfort with you, and thus empowered enough to attack you more than they would a white professor with whom they have no prior social affiliation. These situations can be nightmares, as they reflect the esteem problem in the black community that leads us to feel as though attacking and hurting one another is easier, and thus more satisfying than working collectively to fight black oppression. In other words, Smiley was reflecting the same sentiment held by black men who shoot one another on the street, but stand in collective fear of the racism in America. Aaron McGruder, creator of the popular cartoon, "The Boondocks", would refer to this as "a nigger moment."

Phones were ringing off the hook, as I had friends from California to New York calling and asking "What's wrong with Tavis?" I had no idea, since I don't know Tavis personally. However, because we run in the same circles, I know plenty of people who know plenty of people who know Tavis. One of my great and respected friends, Kyle Bowser, is one of Tavis' best friends. Kyle called me on the phone the day after my commentary about Tavis appeared on the Internet. Going through the blogs of prominent black scholars, I had a chance to see their reactions. Melissa Harris-Lacewell at Princeton University, a woman with whom I often disagree, happened to be incredibly poignant in her critique of Tavis Smiley's behavior.

Melissa angered Tavis by writing a column that asked "Who died and made Tavis King of black America?" I wasn't as direct in my critique of Tavis, but I did have some strong words for him. I didn't want to deliver any commentary on the topic via the major networks, since I honestly feel that there are some conversations black folks need to have behind closed doors. But given that we get several thousand black readers per week on our website YourblackWorld.com, I felt this to be a fitting venue to let the world know how I felt.

I issued a statement agreeing with my friend Roland Martin at CNN, who felt that Tavis was out of line by making such a strong demand on Obama at such a critical time. Yes, Hillary Clinton showed up to The State of the black Union in spite of being on the same campaign trail as Obama, but the fact was that Hillary was well-positioned to win in the upcoming battlegrounds states, Texas and Ohio. Also, Hillary Clinton needed to regain the ground in the black community that was lost when her husband Bill shot himself in the foot. The words out of Bill Clinton's mouth during a prior primary in South Carolina were so vile, that his own "ghetto pass" was revoked immediately. Clinton compared Barack Obama to Jesse Jackson, implying that he was simply a black presidential candidate with no chance to win white voters. While Jesse ran an outstanding campaign, the notion that Obama's fate would be similar to his own was disappointing for many black people to hear. Clinton was no longer one of us, and he certainly was not the "first black president" anymore.

I also felt that Tavis should have been more careful about being too critical of Obama in light of the fact that he was accusing Barack of doing some things that he himself had been doing. For example, Tavis claimed that he was not going to give Obama a "ghetto pass" just because he was black. Rather, he would challenge and question him like he would anyone else.

First, Tavis' attack on Obama presumes that black voters are not smart enough to know whom they can and cannot give the "ghetto pass". No one gives the "ghetto pass" to

Ward Connerly (the guy in California fighting against Affirmative Action) or Condoleeza Rice, so the idea that black candidates get votes only because they are black is a bit silly. A "ghetto pass", should such a pass exist, must be earned, and Obama had earned the love, trust and support of the black community. To presume that people were supporting him just because he is black is an insult to the collective intelligence of the black community.

Secondly, Tavis himself had been long receiving the very same "ghetto passes" he felt black America was unfairly bestowing upon Obama. As powerful and as revolutionary as Tavis' commentary has been on The Tom Joyner Morning Show, the fact that you hear "This was brought to you by Wal-Mart" at the end of each segment reminds you that the message has been diluted by corporate sponsorship. No great black revolutionary in American history has ever been brought to you by McDonald's, Wal-Mart, Wells Fargo, or any of the other corporations that have sponsored Tavis Smiley's forums.

Additionally, there is a clear reality in the life of Tavis Smiley, one that he cannot ignore: the Covenant with black America, The State of the black Union Conference, The "Pass The Mic" Tour, and nearly everything else Tavis has done was created with the express objective of obtaining revenue and profitability for his corporate sponsors. Tavis has sold himself (and I do not use the word "sold" in a negative sense) to white American corporations as the broker of black leadership. He is the man they believe they can go to in order to reach the African-American masses. We are the drugs, and he is the pusher: white corporate America represents the group of teenagers getting high on the profitability of black consumption.

There is nothing wrong with the Tavis Smiley business model. I am not here to say that Tavis has "sold out", for I don't believe he has. We all sell *something* in order to make a living, and even the concept of "selling out" presumes that one has managed the thin line between making a profitable trade, versus giving up something of tremendous value. The problems with the Tavis Smiley business model arise when such a business model is pursued carelessly or selfishly. I do not accuse Tavis Smiley of being careless or selfish. However, his attacks on Senator Barack Obama, none of which were thrust on Senator Hillary Clinton, smelled of self-interest from a man who appeared to feel slighted that Obama jumped his place in the line of great black leadership.

I felt sorry for Tavis after seeing the reactions of our readers on YourblackWorld.com. Hundreds of emails and comments were coming in every day, with many readers claiming that they were once Tavis Smiley fans, but not anymore. Overnight, Tavis went from being incredibly popular, to becoming the Milli Vanilli of social commentary. I can't help but wonder what happened behind closed doors, as I am sure his publisher became concerned that he would no longer sell books. His corporate sponsors were surely aware of the fact that he was not in control of the black audience the way they may have felt he was. I am willing to bet that his life was a mess, at least for a while.

Then there is the Tom Joyner Morning Show. Tom Joyner is one of the baddest brothers in America. I became impressed with Tom when I found out that he began his career in nationally syndicated radio by flying from Chicago to Dallas every single day, doing the morning show in one city and the afternoon show in the other. Tom usually has a smile on his face, and he keeps his audience smiling as well.

But the smile on Tom Joyner's face is not the senseless smile of the Happy Negro. It is a smile built on the idea of entertaining people of color while educating them. I have no problem with Tom Joyner. Tom also has a strong corporate model in place, given that he and Tavis have both been quite successful at getting white American corporations to the table to sponsor their work and venues.

All of the financial support that Tom Joyner and Tavis Smiley get from white America is predicated upon one firm belief in the minds of white American companies: that Tom Joyner and Tavis Smiley are incredibly popular with black people. Tom can make money with mild activism. He boycotts companies that do not spend advertising dollars in the black community, and also takes stands on other issues that are likely to generate strong black support. I wouldn't be surprised if advertising with the Tom Joyner Morning Show is a good way for companies to get off the hook, because many black consumers are not concerned with where companies spend their advertising dollars. If this were going on behind closed doors, some might call it a "shake down". Personally, I simply consider it to be part of the "ghetto pass" being offered to popular African-American media figures. I would argue that a "ghetto pass" can be defined to be any situation in which the group to which you've given so much allows you to escape scrutiny that others in opposing groups might receive. Using that definition, everyone might be eligible to receive a "ghetto pass", even some white people.

The problem is that Tavis Smiley's tirades against Obama were not only coarser than the usual dish offered on Tom's show; they were incredibly unpopular with African-

Americans. Tom Joyner's show is based on saying things that make people feel good. Tavis wasn't making anyone feel good by attacking a man who was arguably the most popular black figure in the entire country.

After seeing Tavis' personal attacks on Obama, I knew it was only a matter of days until Tom and Tavis parted ways. I would have been utterly shocked if Tavis had stayed on as part of the team, since I knew money was the primary motivator for the Tom Joyner Morning Show. So, when I heard Tavis had resigned, I wasn't surprised. In fact, I would not be surprised if Tom and his team pushed Tavis in that direction. I am sure the departure was painful, as Tavis and Tom seem to have become very close through the years.

The experience with Tavis Smiley, Tom Joyner and Barack Obama provides a valuable lesson on wealth transfers and black leadership. It is important when earning money in a capitalist society, that there be consistent accountability regarding who receives money, who is paying money and why the money is being transferred. It is no different from a woman going out on a date with a strange man, fully understanding that if the man offers her a diamond bracelet on the first date, she should not take it. The reality is that when someone gives you something, they expect something back. There's no such thing as a free lunch.

Here is how shows like "The Tom Joyner Morning Show" make most of their money: The media outlet obtains eyeballs (or in this case, ears) and then sells those eyes or ears to corporations wishing to peddle their products to the masses. Black media are selling their awareness of the black community, since many of the corporations providing the funding don't know anything about black people and may not want to know. Many of them don't care much about black folks and the government doesn't make them care. So, this leads every liquor store or cigarette manufacturer to become the first in line to sell things to black people. They have no sense of the "double bottom line" that incorporates community consciousness with the objective of maximizing shareholder wealth. In other words, their goal is to make money, not to care about you or me. How much would YOU care about the black community if you were not black?

To supplement the lack of concern for the black community, few of the key decision-makers for large corporations are black, neither are most of the employees, suppliers and other stakeholders. The expectation is that the black community, like any other, would protect and represent its own interests. The notion that we can expect well-intended whites (or anyone for that matter) to represent our interests is quite flawed. The reality is that power only respects power. In a capitalist society, that power is created through the collection of resources and spending power. If that power is diffused, as it has historically been in the black community, then potentially productive action will have been rendered useless and non-existent.

The State of the black Union, the forum held by Tavis Smiley every year, has a far more disturbing set of circumstances than the typical media outlet. I mentioned earlier that I have no problem with the business model of the Tom Joyner Morning Show, or other shows like it. I also have no problem with the revenue generating model for the Tavis Smiley television and radio shows. However, the State of the black Union is another matter. The forum, as presented by Smiley, has become almost diplomatic in nature. It is meant to be a venue in which policy is

created for the black community and unelected leaders of the community provide guidelines for the implementation of this policy. The forum is designed to provide a head-on-challenge to the oppressive forces that have kept black people as the underclass of American society.
While the State of the black Union is created to be productive, it is also created to be *profitable*. Corporate sponsors abound, most of them being predominantly white corporations seeking to gain visibility and influence within the black community. Many of the corporations allowed to sponsor the venue have been accused of harming the black community by taking the homes of African-Americans through foreclosure, sending urban jobs overseas, or hooking the community on poisonous products such as cigarettes and alcohol.

The State of the black Union, if it is not careful, may become a "financial confessional" in which those firms accused of hurting the black community can make everything right with a donation to Tavis Smiley. There is little reason to invest $100 million dollars into the black communities across America when you can maximize your bottom line by giving $1 million dollars to have Tavis Smiley say good things about you. Engaging in good corporate behavior is far more expensive than simply marketing good corporate rhetoric (that's why they say that "talk is cheap"). Therefore, many companies would rather spend their entire budget marketing their good behavior, rather than paying to actually engage in the good behavior itself.

The attempt to fight oppression via corporate sponsored activism is problematic for another reason. It is very difficult to challenge oppression, while simultaneously maintaining a perfect relationship with your oppressor. Many of the corporations that sponsor The State of the black Union, such as Wal-Mart, have a critical divide between themselves and the black community. African-Americans across the country have protested the activities of Wal-Mart, as the company has been accused of harming many of the communities within which it places its stores. The State of the black Union forum would not be the appropriate venue to challenge such powerful corporate forces, since it would be difficult to explain why Wal-Mart should sponsor a venue that would degrade the public perception of its brand.

To help us understand the inherent contradictions at risk during the State of the black Union, I can use the following example. Imagine if President George W. Bush were to announce that "This year's State of the Union Address is being brought to you buy Mahmoud Ahmadenijad of Iran and Venezuelan President, Hugo Chavez." Given that Iran and Venezuela are political enemies of the United States and do not have the best interests of the US at heart, it would make no sense for President Bush to allow these countries to sponsor important diplomatic forums. While I do not consider American corporations to be the unconditional enemy of black people, there are certainly areas in which corporate America has pursued interests that are in direct conflict with the progress of the black community. So, having an adversarial force sponsoring your important diplomatic initiatives is generally a bad idea, like allowing the cat to guard the fish tank.

Does this mean that the State of the black Union forum should not try to make money? No, it does not. As a capitalist, I applaud Smiley's vision. I applaud the idea of making a profit and using the power of capitalism to create the opportunity for fair and free expression. What I argue is that the nature of corporate sponsorship should be examined carefully. An unbiased committee should be responsible for determining the nature, necessity and incentives of any entity wishing to sponsor the forum. Who gives money, why that money is being given; who receives those funds and the conditions of sponsorship should be carefully considered when accepting financial support. This is no different from a father who carefully inspects any gift a young man gives to his daughter. He would want to know why the young man is giving her the gift, and what he expects in return. It's only common sense.

If Wells Fargo wants to sponsor the State of the black Union after being accused of predatory lending, a powerful effort on the part of this corporation should be required to show that this sponsorship is meaningful. The sponsorship should be supplemented with clear plans to support those in urban centers across America wishing to stay in their homes. In other words, we need campaign finance reform in the black community.

In Corporate Finance, we teach a subject called Agency Theory. Agency Theory analyzes the incentives of firm managers and other stakeholders to determine how those incentives can be misaligned. One thing that happens consistently in Agency Theory is that, in the end, although the firm manager's job is to represent the interest of the shareholders, he does not do this. Instead, the manager does what any other human being does: he takes care of himself.

Secondly, Agency Theory also explains corporate takeovers and something called Managerial Entrenchment. In this theory, the manager is responsible for doing what is best for the shareholder. But again, he does not usually take care of the shareholders the way he should. Instead, he thinks of himself first, shareholders second. So, if one offer to purchase the company pays the shareholders well but does not benefit the manager, his incentive is to pass up the offer. However, if a second offer comes through that takes good care of the manager at the expense of the shareholders, he will take the second offer. In other words, the people the manager is protecting are not as important as the manager's desire to maintain his personal power.

This is the danger of the State of the black Union Conference and it is also a problem that afflicts all of global politics. Corporate sponsors are not dumb. They know that in order to protect their image in black America, they do not have to take care of the black community. They only have to take care of anyone who has put himself in the position to be called a "black leader." This does not, however, imply that all black leadership is corrupt; but the truth is that for any form of leadership, there is always the temptation for corruption. Also, the State of the black Union, while being created to protect and support the black Community was also designed to secure a good income for Tavis and his team (it is difficult to do this sort of thing without making it profitable). Again, earning an income is not a problem in and of itself. But the drug of money must be carefully monitored and regulated.

Agency Theory leads one to question if Tavis Smiley's tirade against Senator Obama was because he truly felt Mr. Obama did not care about black people or if he felt that Obama had disrespected him. This would be no different from a pastor saying "We all need to serve the Lord, as long as it's done in my church."

I am the first to admit that we are all hypocritical when it comes to our financial incentives. Most of us, at some point in our lives, avoid doing the right thing because of some financial concern: an attorney lets an innocent man go to prison because he doesn't want to violate the attorney-client privilege; a college coach allows his star player's mother to remain homeless because he doesn't want to violate NCAA rules against non-payment; a factory worker watches in silence as his colleague is fired for something he didn't do; the list goes on and on. The point is that it is imperative for all of us to at least try to do the right thing, or at least remain aware of when and why we end up doing the wrong thing.

Personally, I like money a lot. I started my career at Syracuse University rather than an HBCU because I had a lot of student loans and I needed to repay them. It wasn't until later that I realized that many HBCUs have been taken over by individuals who don't have much desire to hire African-American scholars. Also, early in my career, I believed the myth that a top researcher should prove himself at a predominantly white university before doing anything else.

I have earned money in other ways during my career: I have taken money for speeches that I would not have given had I not been compensated. Did I care about the issue on which I was speaking? Absolutely. But the truth was that if I didn't pay my own bills, I knew that no one else would.

Later in my career, I realized that predominantly white universities are no better than HBCUs, and I cared less about what others would think if I passed up the chance to teach at an Ivy League institution. Also, I began giving more speeches for free in order to give something to the community. However, my ability to ignore money in my personal choices was afforded by financial security and emotional security. I felt good about who I was, I didn't need external validation from others, and I had some money in my bank account. It takes time to get to that point.

It is for these reasons that I do not fault individuals such as Tavis Smiley.

There are signs when the addiction to money has gotten too strong. There are lines that must be drawn in the sand and a point at which you choose virtue over profitability. I am sure that Tavis and others have their own lines, for I believe Tavis cares about black people. Personally, my line has been drawn by the fact that while I enjoy making money, I never wanted to make too much of it. I have deliberately sabotaged opportunities to be well-compensated by CNN and other networks because I did not want money to corrupt my spirit and allow me to forget what is important.

When I became a public scholar, I promised myself that I would not become famous for the wrong reasons or become indebted to the wrong people. That is why I did not want to appear on Oprah or the other shows that seem to prove that you've "made it big." If I was going to be rich and famous, it was going to be for the right reasons, with support from the right sources.

When I signed with a speakers' bureau, I did not sign with The American Program Bureau, a large, so-called mainstream speakers' bureau that seems to enjoy promoting whichever hot, new black man emerges on the scene. I signed with Great black Speakers; a bureau that I knew would not force me to compromise my blackness. The same thing was true when I wrote my books, since I did not want my voice as a black man to be muted.

Like a drug addict who knows his limits, I promised myself that I would not allow money to cause me to overdose on social irresponsibility. I knew that by keeping myself out of certain situations, I could use money to empower me and not to enslave me. I did not want to survive solely on mainstream corporate sponsorship because I knew that true and pure activism cannot come from the financial belly of most major American corporations. It is not, for one second, within the incentive structure of any American corporation to sponsor black activism. That would make no sense. I assume that Tavis and others know this. If they didn't know it before reading this book, I am sure they know it now.

Chapter 7

Why black People are Broke

I recall reading an article in USA Today that was being circulated around the internet. Apparently, the article was quite popular, since I saw it forwarded to me 2 or 3 times. The article explained, in the author's interpretation, why African-Americans have such little wealth. In the column, the author cited a litany of statistics, from how many billions of dollars African-Americans spent on clothing, to a comparison of the amount of money spent on shoes versus the amount spent on books. For example, the author cites that "In 2002, the year the economy nose-dived; we spent $22.9 billion on clothes, $3.2 billion on electronics and $116 billion on furniture to put into homes that, in many cases, were rented." The article then moved on to conclude that African-Americans are financially irresponsible, with the subtle indication that it is this financial irresponsibility which leads to the financial inequality we see in America.

In other words, the author was saying "black people live in ghettos because they have a trillion dollars and just waste it." While I certainly have no problem with tough love and critical analysis, I found the article problematic and disturbing for several reasons. I will start with the small issues and move to the bigger concerns after that. First, simple raw data on the amount of money spent on a certain commodity is meaningless without putting that data into context. For example, if I say "The United States spent $1 billion dollars on the military last year," that statement may sound quite impressive. The problem is that if the US were to only spend $1 billion dollars per year on its military, we could be taken over by Cuba. Numbers without context mean nothing, so simply stating the raw amount of money African-Americans spend on clothing each year, without comparing that to the total disposable income level, as well as the per-capita amounts spent by other ethnic groups does nothing to prove that African-Americans are excessively wasteful. While the author of the article did make a few comparisons to other ethnic groups, there were some key omissions in the analysis.

The second reason I found the article to be a tad misplaced is because the author apparently did not read, or chose to ignore, much of the data on white American spending, saving, borrowing and investing habits. The article was written to argue that blacks engage in overconsumption, implying that whites have more wealth because they are financially responsible, relatively speaking. The problem is that the author is a bit misguided on this issue. The truth is that white Americans are just as bad as African Americans when it comes to wasting money.

During the summer of 2006, I was a visiting Fellow for the Center for European Economic Research in Mannheim Germany. One day, one of my colleagues came into my office to ask me a question. Speaking with a thick German accent, he simply asked me if there was something wrong with Americans.

I wasn't sure where the question was coming from, so I told him that there was nothing wrong with us. Not to say that he was wrong, but his blunt force attack on my country made me feel a little defensive. He then explained the nature of his question. In the conversation, he stated these simple facts that were discovered during the data analysis of a research study he was conducting:

Germans have lower incomes than Americans do. Germans pay more in taxes than Americans do. Germans save *nearly 5 times more* money than Americans do.

When he gave me this data, I was shocked. I had no idea that Americans were so horribly irresponsible with their money. But after additional reflection, I realized that he was telling the truth. Americans are incredibly wealthy compared to the rest of the world. The problem is that we do not realize just how rich we are. We are a nation that loves excess. Most Americans had never lived through a prolonged financial crisis, until the economic downturn of 2008. We spend twice as much on healthcare as the entire Gross Domestic Product (GDP) of India, a nation with over a billion people. Not having experienced real struggle makes it difficult to imagine the importance of financial frugality.

This excessive tolerance for financial risk is no different from a child who has never felt the burn of a hot stove, enticing him to playfully hover over the stove to get extra cookies. Our willingness to take on added risk shows itself in the decisions by many Americans to buy homes they could not afford during the subprime lending crisis of 2008. Rather than follow rules set on the percentage of disposable income one should spend on a mortgage, we spent whatever we could afford. Credit cards were as readily available as crack cocaine on a street corner, and we were all addicts. Families appeared to be doing well on the outside, but were one paycheck away from homelessness on the inside.

These problems and excessive risk taking were not just present in the black community; they were present throughout all of America. Most Americans don't save.

Many Americans only invest through their retirement programs (if they have them) or through home ownership (if they own a home). But even investments made in home ownership were undercut by borrowing against the value of the home.

At one point, borrowing against the home seemed to be a good bet, because home values were appreciating at a record pace. Alan Greenspan, the former Chairman of the Federal Reserve, was given credit for the growth in housing prices that began in the 1990s. By allowing greater availability of funds via lower interest rates and relaxed monetary policy, Greenspan created what is called a "bubble" in housing prices. Borrowing money is like renting a car, and the car rental fee is the interest paid to borrow that money. Greenspan, by continuously reducing interest rates (as well as other acts he committed as chairman), has been accused of leading the charge toward additional borrowing, seeing as he effectively reduced the cost of money.

At the time, Greenspan's actions seemed to make sense. He was hailed a hero and guru by the American media. The problem is that chickens always come home to roost, and this situation was no different. By making money so cheap and available, Greenspan created a bubble in housing prices that not only made homes difficult to afford, but also created a nation that had become dependent on the increasing value of these homes in order to get by. The bottom line is that when money is cheap, it is easier to leverage your $70,000 income to buy a $280,000 home instead of the $150,000 home you should have considered in the first place. Given that incomes were not rising as high as home values, America was effectively mortgaging and leveraging itself into the ground. As in life, leverage has the upside of allowing you to get more from what you've got, but it's got the downside of additional volatility if things don't go as expected. Not only had many Americans purchased homes they could not afford, they were borrowing against the value of these homes in order to maintain the lifestyle to which they'd become accustomed.

African-Americans are usually body slammed by American financial downturns. The old adage "last hired, first fired" is still true, given that many organizations and institutions only began hiring black folks in serious numbers a few years ago. Many of them still have not done so to this day. So, being at the bottom of the boat means you are the first to drown when the ship starts to sink.

The subprime lending crisis hit hardest in urban centers across America: Detroit, Atlanta, DC, and Chicago. What was most interesting about the crisis was that it didn't just hit the poor. It was hitting the middle class. This was the group who'd allegedly "made it". These were the ones who seemed to be "binging and balling," but they were actually "busted and broke." Many of us carry the false belief that earning $80,000 dollars per year implies that we should have the nicest of everything. Such notions quickly ignore the importance of saving for the future and other critical financial decisions. So, if chickens were coming home to roost in the white community, they were doing a double roost with black folks.

Part of the reason African-Americans were hit so hard during the subprime lending crisis leads me to agree, hesitantly, with the author of the USA Today article mentioned above. As I mentioned before, I don't feel that the author was ill-intended, and I am also a believer in tough love. The truth is that African-Americans do not have much practice with wealth. Historically, we have

79

never earned much money, so there is a perception that once you've "made it," all financial problems and concerns go away and you are free to do what you will with your income.

Added to our lack of financial literacy is a common misperception that a high income implies that you are wealthy. This is not true in general, and is doubly false among people of color. The fact that African-Americans have, to this point, a virtually non-existent legacy of wealth implies that we are far less likely than others to receive an inheritance or to have parents who can bail us out of our financial problems. Our ancestors left us many assets of tremendous value, but because of racism, money was not one of those assets. Additionally, African-Americans are far more likely to have student loans or bad credit, as being on financial thin ice significantly increases the likelihood that you are going to experience financial turmoil.

African-Americans are doubly affected by "financial thin ice": not only are we least equipped to endure a financial crisis, but structural and educational limitations increase the likelihood that a financial crisis is going to occur within our communities. Not having a legacy of wealth implies that you do not have the financial cushions to protect you when things go south. Additionally, structural problems occur in a society that is infected with institutionalized racism, as the best and most secure positions with most American institutions are held by white men. Finally, educational limitations come into play when financial literacy for one ethnic group is weaker than others. When it comes to all three criteria, African-Americans have historically been on the short end of the stick.

An added complication that exists as a result of the factors mentioned is that there is a dual economic reality for middle class African-Americans that does not exist for other ethnic groups. I can explain this complication with an example. I've heard people conduct studies comparing financial habits of African-Americans with other ethnic groups, and of course, the choices are never the same. But in order to accurately compare ethnic groups, those gathering the data attempt to normalize the study by holding income levels constant. At the end, they sometimes make a statement similar to the following: "Holding income levels constant, African-Americans spend 20% of their disposable income on clothing, as compared to 10% for whites."

On the surface, the statement sounds relatively accurate, given that one can say that two individuals, both college graduates, earning $80,000 per year are on the same financial playing field. The problem is that these two individuals may not be on the same field at all.

First of all, income is not the same as wealth. Income is the tip of the iceberg when attempting to analyze an individual's true financial condition. Wealth is a more accurate measure of financial well-being, given that it takes into account the fact that whites are more likely to get an inheritance from their dead grandparents, to receive a $30,000 gift at their wedding, to have their college paid for with no student loans or to have someone bail them out in the event that they make a financial mistake. African-Americans are far less likely to have this kind of support, and it shows in their financial outcomes.

Consider Billy, a good white kid from the suburbs. He is in the same cohort with James, a black child from the city. While we all know that every white kid doesn't live in the suburbs and every black kid doesn't live in the inner city, the reality is that there are still clear statistical socioeconomic disparities that exist at birth.

Billy's dad is a middle manager at Ford and his mother is a counselor at a local high school. Both of Billy's parents are college educated, and middle class. When Billy's grandfather dies, he leaves the family a fully paid $150,000 home, in addition to another $100,000 in stocks and bonds. The value of the home and stock has accrued through years of growth, as his grandfather acquired his first financial asset in the 1930s.

Part of the money is put into Billy's college fund, after the assets are shared with the siblings of Billy's father. These funds exist in addition to the money that his parents have been saving, as well as the money earned through equity accumulation in the family's home.

Billy goes to college debt free and graduates with a degree in business. His father, due to his experience in the field, advises Billy to get an MBA, which he again obtains debt free. After finishing his MBA, Billy's father uses his connections to get Billy a position with IBM as a manager. Billy is a natural fit, since the other IBM managers are also white males. They play golf together, and Billy's mentor notices how Billy reminds him of himself at that age. At the age of 25, Billy decides to get married. As a wedding gift, his parents give him $30,000 toward the down payment of his first home.

Billy purchases the home with his spouse, also a college graduate with middle class parents. Not to be outdone, her parents also provide the family with a few thousand dollars to get started. Years later, equity value accumulates in Billy's home and his net worth at the age of 35 is roughly $200,000. He loves the college he attended, so he gives them a $5,000 donation every year.

He can afford to do this because of the cushion of wealth, education and job security he and his wife have obtained over the years. Additionally, he has no relatives calling to borrow money, since nearly everyone in his family is financially secure. If anyone in the family does endure a financial crisis, everyone can chip in to fix the problem without any one person being hit too hard.

James has a different reality from Billy and thus a different life. James' parents are good, hard working Americans who listen intently to Bill Cosby when he preaches the value of good behavior. So, in spite of the fact that James is born in the middle of a drug infested neighborhood with children being shot on a regular basis, his parents send him to school every day and make James strong enough to avoid the temptations of the neighborhood. His parents never went to college, but they work hard. They were lucky enough to avoid the economic gutting of black communities that took place when the manufacturing base left America in the 1990s, so they have jobs earning a wage good enough to feed their children.

Despite James' dilapidated school, which has far fewer books than Billy's and a far worse graduation rate and teacher-student ratio, the Bill Cosby lessons prevail and James simply finds a way to make it work. His parents don't have much money, but they are wealthy with spirit, and give their child the strength to overcome obstacles that destroy the lives of millions of black youth every year. While James is able to overcome his environment, many of his friends cannot. Some of them, who also chose to do the right thing, end up in circumstances and situations that lead to their demise. As a result, James watches three of his friends die before his high school graduation.

James pushes to gain acceptance into college and decides to attend. His grandfather died last year, but had nothing to leave him. It wasn't because his grandfather was a lazy man. It was because when his grandfather built his career, there were few opportunities for African-Americans to go to college or build wealth. So, in spite of working hard his entire life, he has nothing to leave his children and grandchildren.

James' parents, because they themselves have struggled to stay together and keep their family fed, have little to give James as he starts his journey through life. So, James goes to college with student loans. He works hard in school, earning a 4.0 grade point average while he is in college. He wants to make his life better. The debt mounts, but this doesn't stop him. He graduates from college and then takes additional loans to get an MBA.

After graduate school, James meets Tiffany, a beautiful and ambitious young black woman he has chosen to make his wife. Again, at Bill Cosby's suggestion, James concludes that he is not going to make Tiffany into a "baby's mama", and does the "right thing." The last thing he would want is to give the right wing ammunition as they insult the integrity and value systems of African-Americans by making reference to the rate of unwed births. Sure, they ignore the fact that white America has an equally problematic divorce crisis in its own community. They also ignore the fact that not getting married is probably a wiser choice than getting married and then choosing to damage your child emotionally through divorce proceedings. All that matters is "doing the right thing", even if you are ultimately doing the wrong thing for your children or your own well-being. James makes the right decision by marrying Tiffany, who is beautiful on both the inside and the outside, turning out to be a wonderful wife.

But the family has to struggle. Not only were their parents unable to provide a down payment for the couple's home as a wedding gift, they were even unable to pay for the wedding. So, James and Tiffany, in addition to being saddled with $150,000 in student loan debt, must incur an additional $10,000 in debt in order to get married. To make matters worse, Tiffany's credit is a bit "challenged" because she had to incur massive credit card debt to pay bills during college. The Bill Cosby dream doesn't come cheap. The idea of buying a home is remote, no mortgage company is willing to lend to a couple with this kind of debt level in conjunction with a weak credit score.

So, the new couple puts off buying a home until they are financially prepared to do so. In spite of not being able to buy a home just yet, they are the stars of the family. James and Tiffany's decision to rise above their circumstances and become educationally successful makes their families proud. Bill Cosby would be excited to hear their stories.

But being the star of your family has a downside. While no one works to be a burden on the young couple, the truth is that life happens. James' father dies suddenly, and his mother is left to struggle financially. So, James helps his mother in every way he can. Additionally, James' little brother is going to college and it would make no sense for him to be doing so well without lifting up his sibling. This drains the family's finances a bit more. Additionally, Tiffany has a brother with a drug problem who finds himself homeless on a regular basis. Although she eventually cuts him off, there is family pressure to help her brother. She doesn't want to be a snob, deserting those she loves after obtaining some degree of success.

Years later, James and Tiffany are 35 years old, still sitting under over $100,000 in debt, without a home of their own. Saving has become a challenged afterthought, since all expenses eat into the family income quickly. There is a financial fire to put out every week and it leaves the family drained. Of course it would be easier to just cut everyone off, but cutting off those you love who've supported you for years is not a good, nor Christian, thing to do. So, beyond Tiffany's brother with the drug problem, everyone else gets whatever help the couple can provide.

When Tiffany's HBCU calls to ask for donations, she wants to help. The problem is that she can't; she has already started a charity out of her own home. Not only is she reaching back to help those in her family who are struggling, she is also trying to get into position to purchase her first home and get out of debt. So, giving back to her HBCU is an almost impossible challenge.

So, when the HBCUs do their annual study on giving, their conclusion is that "HBCUs struggle because black alumni don't want to support their universities." This conclusion bothers Tiffany because nothing could be further from the truth. While Tiffany and James would like to give as much as Billy and his wife, the reality is that they are simply not equipped to do so. They have run the race just as hard with just as much energy (actually more energy, because statistics show that Billy would likely never have made it out of James' environment), but where you start the race plays a huge role in how you finish.

The reality is that this disparity exists all across America. There was an old baseball player who once said "Some people were born on third base and swear they hit a triple." The truth is that wealth legacies are the mountain on which you are born, and those who are forced to start building a mountain from scratch will have a tough time ending up just as tall.

I grow weary of hearing those who attempt to argue that economic inequality exists because black people don't work as hard, are not as disciplined as others or do not want to be successful. Laziness, hard work, good values and smart choices know few ethnic boundaries and no group holds a monopoly on work ethic. The truth is that economic inequality exists for one reason and one reason alone: For 400 years, black people were not allowed to participate in the economic growth and prosperity of our country.

Assume you and I are racing our cars across the country. The drive is 6,000 miles driving from New York to California and back. If you travel 60 miles per hour, it will take 100 hours for you to make the drive. Assume I give you a 50 hour head start in the race. By the time I even begin, you will have traveled 3,000 miles already. So, even if I travel 50% faster than you, you are going to beat me in the race by 1,500 miles.

To any observer of the finish who does not know the history of the race, it would appear that you are clearly the better driver. You could stand arrogantly at the finish line, preparing to lecture me on the importance of good racing values, discipline and hard work. You would use your success as a shining example of why I could be successful if I could only drive like you, take the same routes as you and behave like you.
You would be wrong.

America is the same way. Our country has a horrible habit of lecturing black people on good values, the importance of social norms and the reasons that we struggle economically. There is nothing more devastating than when arrogance and ignorance are in the same room together, as you have the likes of Bill O'Reilly and Sean Hannity on Fox News spending their time explaining that black people could be better off if they would just grow up and stop being so stupid. I grew tired of doing interviews with the likes of Bill O'Reilly after hearing him explain that economic inequality was due to the fact that black people do not have good values and black men do not marry the mothers of their children. All the while, he and others mention nothing of the high divorce rates in the rest of America, which have an equally devastating impact on American families.

Rush Limbaugh, the high school graduate who also serves as one of the intellectual leaders of the Republican Party, condemns African-American drug users to prison, while he himself has been hooked on drugs. Given the ridiculous dispositions of many conservatives in this country, it is quite ironic that the intellectual leader of the conservative movement is a recovering drug addict (or so he says) and high school graduate. That will be the legacy of many of the racists in America, for they do our country a grave disservice with their bigotry.

Arrogance comes from white supremacy. It is in the very blood and birth right of many Americans, even those who try their hardest not to be racist. The arrogance of white supremacy is a social disease that infects the core of the existence of millions of Americans. The arrogance shows itself in the way people of color are judged and hyper analyzed by a society that has been trained to hate black people, especially black men.

The ignorance in the room comes from the fact that most of America is incredibly dumb. I have to be straightforward in my assessment and argue that the existence of white supremacy is not due to the fact that people intentionally try to be evil. I believe that most Americans, white, black and otherwise, want to do the right thing by their fellow man and woman. But when one is not properly educated on the history of racial inequality, it is easy for individuals to come to the wrong conclusions. Additionally, when one is born and raised with a sense of entitlement and unapologetic dominance, it can bring out the very worst in our humanity.

When foreigners come to America, many of them have inaccurate perceptions of black people. Even many Africans and Jamaicans come to America and choose not to associate with African-Americans. This is because some of them have a perception that black people are lazy, shiftless, ignorant and violent. These perceptions come from a media that chooses only to focus on negative images of people of color and a public that believes these images to be true. As a result of biased media portrayals, the original sin of white supremacy spreads like a disease to those who are not yet American. Another consequence of these portrayals is the fact that white Americans across our nation and even black people who grow up in the suburbs do wish not to be associated with the negative individuals they perceive to represent the inner city African-American.

During my work with national media, I've noticed that the easiest way for a black man to get on television was to express a willingness to disrespect black people and place the blame for 400 years of slavery and oppression squarely on our shoulders. I am convinced that this is how Juan Williams at Fox News stays employed. Were Juan to utilize a more "fair and balanced" approach to explaining the black experience, I am sure he would no longer have a job.

Going back to the racing analogy used earlier, if I were to watch a cross-country race and see one person cross the line hours before his competitor, my first assumption would be that the winner was a faster, stronger runner; better trained and harder working. If no one were to tell me how the gap was created in the first place, I would never know the difference and promptly give the trophy and pat on the back to the guy in first place. But I might be better informed if someone were to explain the history of the race: who started first, why one person was left behind, and how the guy in second had to overcome far more obstacles than the guy in first. Understanding history might change my response.

Watching without understanding history is not how America analyzes its racial past. White supremacy subtly forbids a deep and realistic analysis of historical racism. Such a study would undermine the perception of America's historical perfection. It would also disrupt the social hierarchy between blacks and whites. Finally, and most importantly, it would force America to embrace the personal responsibility necessary to correct historical wrong-doings. The term "personal responsibility" can be comfortably tossed onto the back of someone else, as long as you are not forced to be responsible enough to use such a term on yourself. America, to some extent, has become the ultimate welfare queen.

Chapter 8

Racism vs. Racial Inequality

I am, in some ways, a relatively naïve human being. I see the good in people because I want to believe that it's there. Although I am not a particularly religious person, I am comforted by the fact that religious doctrine provides meaningful boundaries for decent and humane behavior. I would not want to live in a world where murder was legal, or a man could take another man's possessions just because he was the stronger of the two. I want life on earth to be good and decent, and I truly believe that most of us want the same thing.

Many Americans, really all of us for that matter, are allowed to exist as carelessly as children in a nursery with no concern for the outside world. There is plenty of food, freedom and safety, which gives us the liberty to focus on tiny problems while the rest of the world deals with serious challenges.

In some ways, the lives of most Americans can be compared to that of many academicians. For those in the warm womb of academia, there is very little pressure to prove that your theories actually work in the real world, and little reason to care. You sit in the ivory tower, protected from the rest of the world, and work on research that only needs the approval of your equally insulated colleagues. Some research papers are only read by 5 -10 people and then sit restfully in the dusty archives of some allegedly prestigious journal that grows old and dies in the darkest part of every university library in the nation. The life of an academic is wonderful, especially for white males who run the academy.

I don't fault those who are privileged enough to be oblivious to the rest of the world. To some extent, most Americans, me included, are granted a degree of privilege that we hardly even notice. As much as African-Americans are rightfully outraged over their experiences in America, the truth is that we are incredibly fortunate. Americans are filthy rich compared to the rest of the world, and the reality is that even the poorest Americans are doing incredibly well compared to those in other countries.

Given that most people, in my opinion, are fundamentally good (or at least contain the capacity and desire to do good on some level), it is my belief that most Americans do not choose to be racist. I do not see racism as a conscious choice by the individual, but as a social disease that has been passed from one generation to the next over the past several hundred years. This disease, which affects the mind, is like any other disease that affects the body: the host is not always aware of the presence of the disease and sometimes plays an incredibly passive role in how the disease spreads itself to others.

This is not to presume that individuals do not have the capacity to choose if they are or are not going to be racist. There are certainly periods in which all of us let our political correctness guards down and say things we should not be saying. Again, I include myself in this group. There is also an element of human decency that leads us to make a conscious choice to respect the humanity of other people. At the same time, I stick to the premise that most racism and sexism is relatively unconscious. It also becomes more damaging when we do not make a conscious effort to address the problem.

It goes without saying that a society cannot operate for 400 years with multiple tiers of racial separation and expect that these conditions are going to simply disappear. Most American institutions, from the educational system to the criminal justice system, to economic and prison systems are infected with the disease of racism. The social strata still remain and these disparities do not simply "work themselves out." Like any disease, racism is only cured in a society through a conscious decision to make the patient better.

Anyone who feels that it is a coincidence that prisons are filled with black men is sadly mistaken. Not only are they mistaken, they are making themselves into statistics by simply continuing the same traditions and patterns of ignorance that led us into the social darkness that we must conquer today. It is not a surprise that the educational systems in the inner cities are terrible, while those in the suburbs provide opportunities. We should not be shocked that there is a huge imbalance of wealth and opportunity between individuals based on race. There is no surprise that, after 400 years of unjust racial exclusion by the leaders of our nation, most corporate boardrooms and university halls are essentially devoid of African-Americans.

Insult is added to injury when I am expected, as a black man, to praise and honor individuals who did terrible things to my relatives and ancestors. It's difficult to understand why there is no need to study Malcolm X in public school (beyond the simple stuff), yet I am forced to spend many days and hours memorizing Benjamin Franklin's every move. Much of this double standard is simply the result of the fact that African-Americans, to date, have been the weaker party in racial negotiations.

Those who have the power make the rules, which is true in nearly every other aspect of life.

The outcomes I describe above are not the fault of anyone alive today. They exist by virtue of the fact that some of us have benefited dramatically from the historical aggregation of rape, murder, castration and theft from people of color over several hundred years. In such a case, there should be a conscious effort by our government and individuals in our society to be willing to have the personal responsibility necessary to make things right. It is not only nonsensical, but predictable that there are those arrogant enough to graciously accept all of the benefits of white privilege, and then immediately reject the consequences of it. That is no different from a man getting a loan from a bank, spending the money and refusing to repay the debt. That person would be called a dead-beat.

So, to some extent, our nation has become a dead-beat when it comes to dealing with the realities of disparities it has created through behavior of the past. We accept the benefits that came from the American Revolution, industrialism, and World Wars I and II. We also accept the benefits that came from slavery. America was BUILT on slavery, as any nation allowed to compete in the world economy with free labor would surely have an advantage. It was this advantage that led to the United States obtaining such economic dominance over the rest of the world. In other words, much of the economic greatness of America was truly built on the backs of African-Americans. People often speak to me about the fight against racism. When I am on shows with Reverend Al Sharpton, the tone of his discussion is usually one that focuses on the fight against racism as part of the tradition of Dr. Martin Luther King, Jr. I have no problem with the fight against racism, as that fight is very important. But the truth is that racism is not my greatest concern in the battle for black equality.

I don't worry about someone coming to my office and hanging a noose on my door. I've rarely, if ever, had someone call me "nigger" on the street. I don't worry about not getting service at a lunch counter because of the color of my skin. Not only are such events relatively rare, they just don't bother me all that much.

What I do notice is that while racism does not appear to be a dominant force in the hearts and minds of most Americans, the stench of racism from the past exists all around us. The very fabric of our society was built on a racist foundation, created, perpetuated and dogmatized by individuals who felt, to their very core, that African-Americans were inferior human beings. Therefore, racism is not the greatest problem; rather, RACIAL INEQUALITY becomes the greater demon in our struggle for fairness.

Racism is the input, racial inequality is the output. Imagine a company that goes to a lake every week and dumps thousands of gallons of toxic waste into the water. Assume the company does this for a period of 400 months. Then, one day, the head of the Environmental Protection Agency (EPA) gets wind of the company's activities and decides to do something about it.

The EPA would first respond by telling the company to cease and desist from all dumping activities. The losses must be stopped before you do anything else. There is then the point where the EPA would send environmental experts to assess the damage that has been done. They would visit the polluted, smelly, infested water and take lab samples. They would make a note of all the dead fish and wildlife that have suffered as a result of the company's dumping. They would note the impact on the air around the lake and the drinking water in local neighborhoods. They would also do an assessment of just how long it would take for the lake to be cleaned up.

Finally, they would issue an order to the company regarding how they can rectify the wrongdoing. The company cannot simply say "We've stopped dumping, isn't that good enough?" Such a response would be considered ridiculous, irresponsible and perhaps even criminal. The truth is that *every mess must be cleaned up*. Even if the current CEO was not in charge when the initial dumping took place, she would be well-aware that there have been long-term benefits to the company's profitability, competitiveness and capitalization as a result of the firm's illegal activities. Therefore, the only logical conclusion is that the company should use some of this capital to repay its debt to society.

There are many in America who have reaped the benefits of racism, as well as the substantial long-term benefits to capitalization, inheritance and land ownership. These individuals owe a debt to society. However, rather than forcing the individual to pay his or her debt, the government is the only entity that aggregates resources in such a way that repayment is possible. Racial inequality is the polluted lake that has resulted from 400 years of dumping socioeconomic toxins into American society. There were very serious long-term financial and social benefits from the use of immoral and sometimes illegal activity to gain an advantage in business and industry. Most American corporations are run by whites. Most American universities are run by whites. Major media is controlled by whites. All of this resulted from the use of slavery and oppression to exclude African-Americans from the opportunity to control and access capital in America. There was a 400-year socioeconomic pillaging of a group of people, and modern day racial inequality is the child born from the actions committed in the past.

Racial inequality, like the pollutants in the lake mentioned above, is not going to go away just because people have chosen not to be racist anymore. The racism that exists in the hearts and minds of some today is only a tiny drop in the bucket of long-term pain, inequality and social dysfunction created by the actions of the past 400 years. The reality is that our nation must engage in the personal responsibility necessary to properly pay its debt to the American people. That debt is one which is clearly owed to African-Americans, who've spent hundreds of years building this nation but were not properly compensated for their labor.

Racism does still play some role in today's society. It even shows itself in how people respond to race-oriented conversations. One example is when some argue that the mere mention of racism as a factor in the structure of American society constitutes "whining" and "race baiting." I am not angry when people use these terms, for they've been taught by white supremacy to think in this way. A similar reaction would come from a wealthy man who doesn't want to be reminded that his wealth came from the crimes of his father. The beneficiary of the crimes, who may also play a role in perpetuating the very same attitudes and institutions that led to the crimes being initially committed, may have acquired a "false harmony" with the descendants of the victims (who may even work for him). The problem is that this harmony is built on a social imbalance created because the past wrongs were never corrected.

None of us enjoy being held responsible and accountable for events we would rather forget. We are tempted to find

97

any slimy excuse to avoid the blame, like a defendant in a criminal trial. "He pulled the trigger, not me," or "Why should I be held accountable for the fact that my brother stole something and then gave it to me?" The very same individuals who do not want to be held accountable for the wrong-doings of the past love accepting and celebrating credit for the wonderful things that their ancestors did. Adding further insult to injury, descendants of the victims are forced to celebrate the ancestry of the perpetrators – Black kids in American schools study and practically worship men from the past who owned slaves. This, folks, is oppression. Such attitudes are not only hypocritical; they are highly irresponsible and unpatriotic. Anyone who wants America to be strong should be willing to force America to work through the demons of its past.

To make matters worse, the arrogance and irresponsibility of racial deniability is founded on a platform of ignorance. Even good people who want to do the right thing are led to do the wrong thing because previous generations chose to create learning environments that only sell illusions about America's past. We tell every terrible story in the world about Hitler (which is justified) and proclaim him to be the devil for killing Jews, yet we do not mention the many millions killed during the Great black Holocaust of the past 400 years. In fact, many of the individuals most responsible for killing and enslaving African-Americans are presented as American heroes.

The rest of the world understands how warped our society is. That is why The United States has been held accountable for its behavior and called a hypocrite by the rest of the world. We worked during World War II and the Vietnam War to free others from oppression, while we kept oppression safe and sound on our own borders and shores. We fight terrorists around the world, yet we've harbored government-sponsored terrorists on American soil for several hundred years.

Again, I feel that most Americans want to do the right thing. Refusing to do the right thing is not necessarily the same as doing the wrong thing. However, refusing to do the right thing certainly allows the inequities of the past to live into perpetuity. American universities, corporations, schools and prisons are all infected with racism from the past. I go down the hall every day on a campus that rarely gives tenure to African-Americans and "ghettoizes" the black faculty by only giving them tenure in African-American studies departments. When I am the one to bring up this issue in public, I am accused of "race baiting," which is another term designed to excuse the perpetuation of racist institutional norms. I understand the nature of these attacks, for the disease of racism is most likely to impact those who think they've been cured. In my case, the liberals on my campus are the ones who feel that they are superior to southern racists due to their enlightenment on social issues.

Racism is the input, racial inequality is the output. Even if we are doing the right thing, it is imperative that all Americans fight against racial inequality.

Chapter 9

Capitalism Gone Wild Exhibit A – The Bob Johnson Effect

I once gave a speech at Stanford University for the black Student Union. We were going to talk about educational empowerment and "black people stuff." The Stanford University campus possesses, as expected, some of the more brilliant minds in America. It also has its share of stuffiness and elitism, as many campuses do. I personally believe that education is what you make of it. A person at a community college who studies for 10 hours a day is, in my opinion, far more capable than a student at Harvard who studies four hours a day. The key to your greatness lies inside your heart, not in the walls of the institution you attend.

One of the heads of the organization showed me around campus, which looked far different from what I expected. I thought I would see grand halls around every corner. Instead, I saw a series of tiny little buildings that looked like the ugliest parts of some random state university. Only NYU has a campus with a greater mismatch between the prestige of the brand and the actual look and feel of the physical campus. One of the more interesting buildings on the Stanford campus was a building called "The black House."

"The black House" was descriptively named as the place where black students and faculty spend a great deal of their time. Not everyone goes to "The black House," because some black students are not comfortable associating with other black people. That never made much sense to me, but that's just the way things are. It was a tiny building, far less impressive than I expected. But then again, my tour of Stanford got me accustomed with disappointment. This is not meaning to insult Stanford University, which I consider to be right up with Spellman and Morehouse in terms of producing a strong academic environment.

I noticed that there was a lounging area within "The black House," where students would meet for weekly discussions. One of the more recent topics of discussion covered what the students called, "Booties, Exploitation and Thugs," otherwise known as BET. I laughed when I heard the acronym so eloquently created by the students, since we all know that BET stands for "black Entertainment Television."

Bob Johnson, the founder of BET and one of the wealthiest black men in America, has been the subject of at least two decades worth of controversy. I am sure Bob has no problem with the controversy, since every rich, famous and powerful person in America knows that a stack of haters comes along with any successful life. Even I understand his ability to ignore the haters, since I have plenty of haters of my own.

Johnson's network, in all its beauty, could have been one of the great capitalist achievements in the history of black America. Instead, it turned out to be one of the most riveting textbook cases of capitalism gone wild. Either way, we can learn a great deal from the tradeoffs made by Bob Johnson as he rode the backs of his people all the way to the top.

As an ambitious young man, Johnson challenged all of the cable networks to realize that they were not properly serving their communities by offering enough diverse programming. He was speaking for people of color, demanding that there be a network on the airwaves to represent the views and interests of the black community. This kind of initiative is what leads to change. It is also the type of initiative that can breed self-interest. Either way, it was effective, as Johnson made a very clear point that remains true to this day: African-American interests are not reflected in so-called "mainstream" media.

That is when BET was born.

I am not sure when BET went downhill, but I know that the drop was fast and furious. I love hip hop and I even love the sight of a sexy woman. But I quickly found myself wondering why I could turn on BET nearly any hour of the day and see some woman in a bikini dancing to hip hop music. Johnson was a true capitalist and worked hard to maximize shareholder wealth. He realized that original programming was both expensive and risky. He also realized that African-Americans love hip hop music. Rap music videos were both entertaining and cheap, since the network did not have to pay a dime to create the videos. Artists and labels had no choice but to front the cost of the video, since they were badly in need of media outlets to release their content to the public.

Advertisers don't care why eyeballs are on the screen, they only care that they are there. BET guaranteed eyeballs by showing rap music videos nearly 24 hours a day, and the advertisers came in droves. High revenue with low cost was the simple formula that made Johnson rich.

Bob Johnson has been demonized, rightfully, for his role in creating a generation of youth who memorize "Lil Wayne" rap lyrics before learning their ABCs. What is also appalling is that Johnson's buddy, Bill Cosby, stands first in line to criticize black youth for their behavior, while not holding the primary pusher, Johnson, responsible for doping up the minds of our kids.

But while Johnson was certainly the perpetrator in this great crime against black America, he was also a victim. Bob Johnson, to some degree, can be considered a victim of the fact that a capitalist society tends to judge people by the amount of money in their bank accounts, and not by how that money actually got there. The man with the most money has the most power and thus the most respect and prestige. After the words "How much money did you say he has?" ring into the air, all sins are usually forgiven.

Ebony Magazine, Essence and black Enterprise are also culprits in this great crime, as they are quick to create lists of "The Most Powerful black Men in Hollywood" and "The Richest black People in America." Such lists and the respect that comes with them are problematic in the sense that wealth, power and popularity are the status symbols of the day, and it can be difficult for African-Americans to obtain any of these things without engaging in activities that lead to the erosion of black culture and institutions. Effectively, we become a nation of prostitutes bragging about who made the most money the night before.

Three primary sources of prominence in a Capitalist Democracy are money, power and popularity. African-Americans tend to have a dearth of all 3 of these highly valued resources. It is natural to want these three things, because such pursuits lay at the core of human nature. The problem is that when the winner of the game is the one who has the most money, we can all become as myopic and one-dimensional as a group of teenagers.

Power, in a democracy, is largely obtained through voting or financial strength. The fact that we are less than 13% of the American population also implies that we do not have the votes to put our own officials into office and must struggle to have an impact on American politics. Our weak legacy of wealth puts us in a difficult collective financial position, in spite of the strong spending power in the black community. The truth of the matter is that it is going to take some time for us to go pound for pound with white America when it comes to money or votes, so we've got to obtain progress in any way we can.

Bob Johnson, Barack Obama, and Oprah Winfrey are examples of African-Americans who have achieved tremendous heights in money, power and popularity. Johnson is worth over $1 billion dollars. Obama is one of the greatest political leaders in American history. Winfrey is loved by much of America and considered one of the most beloved women on earth.

What is most interesting is that in spite of the achievements of Johnson, Winfrey and Obama, they are tiny on the playing field of American power and politics. Bill Gates could spend $10 million dollars a day, every day, for the rest of his life and still have more money than Oprah Winfrey. Barack Obama, or any black president, would have a difficult time implementing true change in the black community while being surrounded by 300 million Americans who have little reason to respect civil rights.

What Johnson, Obama, and Winfrey also have in common is that they each made tremendous sacrifices in order to obtain their power. Sacrifices are necessary for any meaningful endeavor, but sacrifices at the expense of the black community should be measured carefully.

Bob Johnson, for example, has probably cost the black community several billion dollars in lost productivity because of his work with BET. This does not include the opportunity cost of what the community might have gained had he not run away from the word "education" in his business plan. While he might argue that he was forced to show music videos all day because he was being asked to maximize profitability, the reality is that he could have easily earned several hundred million dollars for his personal bank account (rather than a billion) by balancing his programming with something more productive. It was his allegiance and loyalty to the beast of pure capitalism that led him to cross a line that was ultimately detrimental to the community.

In fact, Aaron McGruder, the controversial creator of the hit cartoon series, "The Boondocks" joked in an episode about BET that BET's motto is "We hate black people." The episode was subsequently banned from television, but was quite funny nonetheless. It is our obsession with capitalism, in its purest form, which leads many of us to praise Johnson the same way that some people might praise a drug dealer who gives away turkeys at Thanksgiving. As if being a multimillionaire was not enough, Johnson had to become a billionaire. He probably never even realized that he had a choice.

Barack Obama wanted to become president. Being a high ranking, highly respected African-American is not enough for most ambitious politicians. Most great men like Obama want to be the HNIC (Head Negro in Charge). Why it was necessary for him to be president, I am not quite sure. There is a point at which he could surely do more good for the black community by being a straight-forward, hard working politician than by being President of the United States. But we are fed the dream. The dream is that by crossing over and achieving the same wealth, power and respect as whites, and being admired by whites, we have somehow transcended the limitations of our blackness and have done something worthwhile. This ambition is no different from a father who feels that loving his own children is not enough. So, he goes out to become the head of a corporation, neglecting his children in the process.

Most of us don't realize that we have a choice in terms of where to "draw the line." The US Government draws the line on corporate profitability by not allowing certain industries to be controlled by foreign governments. This is an important aspect of national security, for those who control key industries have a great deal of power during critical times. There are many American celebrities and athletes who don't feel the need to succeed overseas, despite the fact that they can earn more money that way. The same can be true of African-Americans with a strong commitment to the black community. "Crossing over" is not always necessary, especially when the cost of crossing over becomes extraordinarily high. I am not one to judge this personal choice, but I am adamant about all of us remembering that there *is a choice.*

Since Barack Obama couldn't get enough black votes to reach his personal prize of being President of the United States, he found himself making a litany of compromises in order to reach his goal. He was forced, by American racism, to disown several black men associated with him who've spoken honestly on race, such as Louis Farrakhan and Jeremiah Wright. He didn't show up at the 40th anniversary of the assassination of Martin Luther King, Jr. I saw segments on Fox News during which Michelle Obama, Barack's beautiful, Princeton educated spouse, was referred to as his "baby mama," and a political liability. There were even correspondents on Fox News who made jokes about killing Obama and what a joy it would be.

Personally, I found the coverage to be an outrage. If this was the price we had to pay in order to get into the white House, I wasn't willing to pay it. A woman can't be willing to get naked with a man just to get another date, and the black community should not be willing to give in to the demands of a selfish, racist culture just to achieve the validation of making it into the white House.

Obama did everything in his power to appease the white community, for they held the keys to his dream. In the end, the question remains whether or not the attainment of such a dream would truly have a favorable long-term impact on the status of black people in America. When Obama attempted to "be a black man" and have an honest conversation on race, he saw votes going out the window. Political support plummeted because America was not ready to talk about race.

I am not one to fault Obama for attempting to become president, for I think his achievement was remarkable. But for those with a strong black identity, there is the question of whether or not being President of the United States is more significant than becoming President of Morehouse College. I personally feel that both positions are equally worthy of respect. I have never seen a white man feel inadequate for not having achieved respect and recognition from the black community. However, African-Americans feel a hunger to be validated by white America, and this validation often comes at a price that is difficult to pay.

Finally, there is Oprah Winfrey, America's favorite soccer mom who never actually became a mom (not that this is a problem though, she's been pretty busy). Oprah wanted to be a billionaire, and she wanted to be powerful. Black people don't have enough money to give Oprah the billions she wanted to earn, so she felt the need to expand her message to white women. When Oprah decided to stand with Barack Obama, rather than Hillary Clinton, her popularity plummeted. Clearly, Oprah and her financial backers were disturbed by her decline in popularity and were willing to do anything to help her regain the lead in the race for daytime ratings. Oprah seemed to perform the balancing act quite well, by taking a stand in favor of Obama, yet maintaining her position as the most powerful celebrity in America, according to Forbes Magazine.

The question that Oprah and others must continue to ask is "how much is enough?" Is the entire measuring stick for a talk show host's respectability completely predicated on how much money, power and popularity they have in their possession? This tradeoff would be an easy one in a world in which a strong black identity were not crucial for survival. The problem is that we continue to live in a nation that has not yet learned to accept us for who we are. Were black habits, cultural norms and values respected by all of America, then "crossing over" would not be a matter of crossing over at all. We would all simply be Americans and have enough common ground to avoid subtly insulting one another in the quest for cultural dominance.

Martin Luther King had a dream. That dream, while diluted by American history books, did focus on the idea of "judging someone by the content of their character rather than the color of their skin." During a national TV show, I was asked if I felt that Dr. King's dream had been realized. I answered "Absolutely, but not really." Americans are, for the most part, over the idea of skin color. Instead, the focus is on character. The problem is that the racial inequality created by centuries of cultural dominance has led to an imbalance of power when it comes to determining the skin color of the individuals granted the privilege of evaluating another person's character. The norms and values of white America are preferred and stand as gate keepers to vital resources in media, corporate America and academia. Therefore, when norms and values that we are comfortable with as African-Americans are judged by white Americans, those norms are often times rejected. Jeremiah Wright and Louis Farrakhan are perfect examples. While many African-Americans do not agree with Wright or Farrakhan, they hardly consider these men to be the villainous social outcasts portrayed by the white American media. Therefore, the cultural dominance of one group over another, when highly correlated with skin color, is a perfect example of racism in action. Some would call it "institutionalized racism."

I love Oprah Winfrey. Few have done more for the good of our society and the world as Oprah, and she is among the top 10 people I respect the most on this planet. Also, there is nothing wrong with having a show like Oprah's. One problem, however, is that by successfully crossing over into white America, Oprah gets far more respect from African-Americans than other amazing black women, such as Dr. Julianne Malveaux, who have remained connected to causes in the black community. The point in this discussion is the following: all of us sell something in order to reach our goals. But while we all sell something, few of us should be willing to SELL OUT. Selling out means that you are willing to give up everything you have in order to get a little more success. If this were the case, women would sell their children, little girls would all become prostitutes, and men would be willing to murder their neighbor to get his/her resources. I do not consider

Oprah Winfrey to be a sellout. I simply recommend that every American know where they should personally draw the line.

All items that matter most within the context of your value system should serve as your measuring stick for success, as well as your capital for investment. African-Americans, because we have adopted the idea of using money, power and popularity as our all-encompassing, unrelenting, three-dimensional measuring sticks for black success, have found ourselves selling everything we can in order to obtain these valued resources. In exchange, we surrender everything we hold valuable, such as the health of our community, our love for one another, educational achievement, etc.

What is more disturbing is that the assets we use as measuring sticks are the ones that we have the most trouble obtaining: money is rare for us, and we don't have the population numbers to sustain significant political power. Being "righteously black" is not exactly popular or going to win awards in the white community. So, we are ultimately fighting a battle we may not be able to win. The choice, for many African-Americans, becomes "cash or culture?" White America, for its challenges, usually leaves the door wide open for any African-American willing to let go of his or her cultural values to get a little more money and success. The question is whether or not we are willing to let go of who we are in order to obtain that success. For those who've been raised and acclimated in white culture, there is little tradeoff. The hurdle is as high as convincing a man who loves football to put on a helmet. For those who were raised with a strong black identity, the tradeoff can be both disturbing and Herculean. But for many African-Americans, having the desire to dedicate your life and give everything in order to obtain resources that are rare in your community leaves you both depleted and unfulfilled.

The scene I describe above can be further illustrated by this example: a mother wants her short, chubby children to grow up as good Christians with lots of academic success. However, she doesn't realize that her love for basketball is witnessed by the children in the household as well. So, even though she preaches that education and Christianity are the values she holds dear, she gives extra attention and praise to her son who plays on the basketball team. The other children, who know that actions speak louder than words, follow suit. They stop studying and going to church in order to spend more time on the basketball court. They too want the attention that comes with athletic success, and subsequently allow their studies and faith in God to suffer because of it.

What's worse in the example above is that the children are short and chubby, so they are not likely to have strong careers in professional sports. But they do all they can, including taking steroids and dedicating their lives to practicing sports because they know that athletics is their avenue to admiration in the home. It is this warped value system that leads to these children creating lives for themselves that their mother never envisioned.

Members of the black community are like the children in that house. We speak of black pride, education and taking care of the community, but few individuals truly hold these values dear. What really gets the greatest respect in the black community is having a lot of money, fame and power. Ultimately, it is also white validation via institutional affiliations, media exposure or massive wealth that achieves the greatest degree of respect from people of color. In other words, a black man who is CEO of IBM

111

will always get more respect from the community than a black man who runs a youth center. This would be true even if the CEO of IBM has sold his soul to become successful. Only those with strong black identities will perceive the individual who works with the youth center to be the more successful of the two.

Barack Obama was not a serious presidential candidate until he won the primary in Iowa. Once whites saw him as their possible president, many African-Americans felt they had been "given permission" to support him. Many of the top black scholars in America are forced to teach at predominantly white universities because even their black colleagues will give them less respect for teaching at an HBCU.

The value systems I describe above are accurate, but warped and disturbing. The truth is that loving oneself is incredibly difficult for an individual or group of people who've been oppressed. Deep down, one can develop a love and respect for his oppressor that leads him to, partly out of fear; seek the validation of that oppressor. African-Americans are afraid of the backlash from white America, for good reason. Angering white America and thus experiencing its wrath can cause us to lose the things that we value the most: Money, power and popularity. Barack Obama would feel less important without being a powerful politician. Oprah would feel less significant if her show had one million viewers per day instead of five million. Bob Johnson would feel like less of a man with $100 million dollars in net worth instead of a billion.

It is my argument that individuals in the black community should be judged by their possession of commodities that we hold in high abundance: character, integrity, intelligence and commitment to the black community. It is also important that we learn to judge one another by the commodities that serve as the most valuable resources for our community's improvement. While money and power certainly improve a community, wealth and power mean nothing if the individual possessing these assets is either enslaved, selfish or disconnected. Perhaps judging black billionaires by their net contribution to the inner cities of America can create a higher standard for these individuals. Black television show hosts can be judged by how well their programming supports issues that connect to the black community. All of these changes, little by little, can allow us to progress in American society without being smothered by the pressures of assimilation.

Many of us already work hard to assimilate and even consider it a weakness if you do not have the ability to do so. A child who grows up, lives and dies in "the hood" is going to be judged far more harshly than a white kid who is born, lives and dies in the suburbs. The reality is that Bill Cosby is right about there being a higher standard to which we must adhere. However, the essence of human nature and mere statistical realities indicate that not all of our kids can be above average. Also, some kids are simply not willing to assimilate in order to be successful. Perhaps we should not fault them for that.

Some elements of hip hop can be used as a good example. Crossover appeal is not what makes a hip hop artist strong in all circles. Rather, many artists obtain a loyal support base due entirely to the nature of their music, and the degree to which that music connects to hip hop culture. That is what makes rappers like Common so well-respected. The same can be true for individuals involved in business, law, scholarship and other areas. While crossover appeal is certainly valuable for some things, we must be clear about what we gain and lose when we completely embrace integration and dilution of purpose in our advancement as a people.

When it comes to diversity and integration, I have some critics. I created a website called YourblackWorld.com, a site for African-Americans. YourblackWorld.com was created in response to my experience with mainstream media, which typically provides a one or no-dimensional perspective to black points of view. Although I have a PhD in Finance, I was never called by CNN, FOX or CBS to discuss money or financial issues. I was usually called whenever they had a conversation about "black stuff".

The fact that they saw me as a black man before they could see anything else was no fault of my publicist. A wonderful and energetic woman, my publicist called all the major networks to introduce me as a person well-qualified to discuss the economy, money management, stock markets or global finance. I have trained literally thousands of Suzie Ormans and Wall Street experts through the years, so it was only logical that this be an area that I speak on as a public scholar.

The problem was that many Americans do not see a black man when they envision a financial expert. When they think of black men, many Americans see a rapper, athlete or criminal. At best, they see a black scholar willing to discuss black rappers, athletes and criminals. That became my role with CNN.

I don't mind discussing black people, for I have a very strong black identity. However, the limitations of my role bothered me a great deal, and what bothered me most was that it didn't bother anyone else. If anyone else was upset, it was for all the wrong reasons. I remember having a debate with a black conservative on CNN regarding why African-Americans have such a negative image in the world. The conservative, buying into some of the basic tenants of white supremacy, truly believed that the reason black Americans have such a negative image throughout the world is because black people simply choose to behave like criminals. He argued that if black people would simply mind their manners and stop getting arrested so much, the media would have nothing to report. Apparently, this man had forgotten that there are over 30 million black people in America. So, even if 95% of these individuals were to choose to become perfect angels (or engage in what I call "The Good Negro Behavior Protocol"), there will, by simple statistical fact, be at least 1 million individuals doing things that could embarrass the rest of the community. By virtue of the fact that the media's lens focuses most on those individuals in the black community who engage in embarrassing behavior, it would be these 1 million individuals who receive the most airtime.

I strongly believe in the idea of freedom. I believe that the black community has the right to be as diverse as any other group of people in America. Rappers have as much a right to exist as professors do. The idea that we can get angry at rappers because CNN and other networks focus on rappers more than anyone else is not the fault of the artists, but rather, due to the one-dimensional perspectives of the networks themselves. It's not a matter of who is in front of the camera; it's where the camera is being pointed.

Another problematic dimension to the "good negro behavior protocol" is this idea that all of us should be "embarrassed" when there is a black person on TV behaving in a comical or criminal fashion. I hear educated African-Americans speak of how embarrassed they are by the behavior of Flavor Flav, the ex-rapper turned reality

TV star. I personally find Flavor Flav to be funny and I feel that he has as much of a right to be himself as the white guys on the great MTV show "Jackass." I have never once heard a white man say that he is embarrassed for the white population because of what the guys on "Jackass" do on television. I have never once heard a white female say that she is embarrassed for the white race when Paris Hilton is arrested for drunk driving for the 1,000th time.   The reality is that they know clearly that Paris Hilton and Jackass do not represent the white experience or dominant white expression.

For some reason, black people are the opposite. Rather than questioning why the media gives us an 'either or' reality for how we express ourselves in media, we get angry at one another for choosing to express ourselves in a unique fashion. The truth is that Flavor Flav has a right to be a comedian; he has a right to behave like an ass. If anyone in the world watches VH-1 and thinks that all African-Americans behave like Flavor Flav, then their ignorance is their problem, not mine.

It was this experience in media that led me to use the Internet to find alternative channels to express an empowered and honest message about the black experience. Eventually, I turned away from mainstream media networks (although I still make limited appearances), as we found that our reach within the black community was stronger, more permanent and more empowered when we reached them through the web. The truth was that I only worked with mainstream media in the beginning in order to obtain the legitimacy that black people give one another when we are accepted by the white community. That is also part of the reason I took my first job with Syracuse University, even though I wanted to start my career at an HBCU. I knew that there were some black people who would not listen to my opinions just because I am an educated black man. Rather, they would listen to me because white America was also listening to me. In some ways, I was like Barack Obama, who had to win Iowa before black Americans thought he was a winner. So, the truth is that the same biases I discuss in this book also exist in my own heart. We are all affected by the disease of racism and white supremacy, and I am no exception.

Some have argued that by creating websites like YourblackWorld.com and focusing on black news that I am "being racist." I find terms like "reverse racism" to be a comfortable and convenient form of expression by those who don't understand how racism works. The need to create ethnocentric organizations like YourblackWorld.com is similar to the experience a battered spouse might have in an abusive marriage. The abuser may feel that everything is fine, since he/she sits where they want, does what he/she wants and doesn't get any resistance in the process. The liberation and freedom of the dominant party ends up being at the expense of the abused. The abused member of the relationship must make his or her needs secondary to those of the abuser, and must always walk on pins and needles when the abusive spouse is in the room.

When the abused party liberates herself by leaving the relationship with dignity to get a home of her own, there is going to be resistance. The abuser might say "Why did you leave? We have a good thing going here!" The abused woman is then going to remind her abusive husband of all the requests for equality that she's made in the past, and that her abusive husband has always wanted his wife to remain in the relationship to serve as a secondary support mechanism for the his terroristic agenda.

In America, African-Americans have always been part of the American family. But we have always been the underbelly of that family, the abused step-child. America was built on our backs and has come to depend on our presence, but has never given a damn about our interests. We find ourselves arguing for fairness until we are blue in the face, only to find that the interests of white males are preserved, while those of women and people of color are consistently pushed to the side. Universities admit black basketball players but don't hire black coaches. Corporations hire black secretaries, but not black CEOs. Prisons admit black inmates, but don't hire black wardens. Black people typically find themselves on the short end of institutional sticks created on a foundation of historical bias and inequality.

It is inequality which leads us to start our own "stuff." That is also why we must have our own "stuff" in this Capitalist Democracy. In other words, the art of black institution building must be embraced by our community.

My mind is trained to ignore the calls of "reverse racism" by those who feel that fighting for fairness is an unfair process. The problem is that in order to correct a historical imbalance, it is only logical that you must regain balance by pushing for an imbalance in the other direction. That is how you make things fair again.

Through time, mild segregation of African-Americans can achieve the goal of creating a respectful relationship between white America and the African-American community. By having our own institutions, financial and otherwise, we can then come back to the negotiating table with the rest of America in a position of equal footing. We would no longer be consumers and workers for major corporations; we would be managers and owners. Like the abused wife who must leave the relationship to find her self, we could come back to the marriage and make the marriage stronger, fairer and healthier than it was when one party simply dominated the other. But the fundamental necessity in such a process is for both parties to let go of the old relationship: the abuser has to stop feeling dominant and the abused has to refuse to be dominated. It takes time to achieve this form of parity in America, where dominance and inequality took several hundred years to create. In other words, it's going to take a lot of work to fix the problem.

Chapter 10

The Destruction of American Urban Centers

When I speak around the country, I get a chance to see the trends that are occurring across the nation. The economy in the United States has changed a great deal since the advent of globalization, and it is changing the way companies do business. Policies implemented during the Bush and Clinton Administrations have created avenues for the rich to get richer, mostly at the expense of the American worker. I have never been a fan of "trickle down economics", since there usually isn't much of a trickle without sufficient government intervention. Governments should certainly invest in making businesses strong, because businesses create jobs and ultimately guide the prosperity of a capitalist society. But the problem is that the Corporate Monster is a greedy one, and if it goes unregulated, it will suck and drain all available resources, dropping those resources into the hands of company shareholders.

At the other extreme, socialist norms that focus on redistributing wealth into the hands of the poor do not always lead to the most efficient uses of capital (Zimbabwe's outrageous inflation problem during 2008 – 2009 is a prime example). The poor and uneducated, unfortunately, tend to use a larger share of their wealth toward consumption, rather than investment. Therefore, focusing solely on the poor and/or the uneducated should not be the primary investment channel of a federal or state government. Only a balanced approach creates jobs while maintaining workers rights and the other essentials of a free and prosperous society.

Sustained and controlled capitalism, while inducing some element of greed, can also produce a natural and healthy regeneration that leads to economic prosperity for everyone. Trickle-down economics, in theory, can produce this prosperity, but the problem is that corporations have to do the right thing. We all know quite well that most corporations don't do the right thing unless they are forced to do so.

To help you see the issue more clearly, we can construct an example. Assume that a mother has $10 to give to her children. Each of them demands a fair distribution of five dollars apiece. The older sibling, who has learned how to start a business in middle school, wishes to invest in a lemonade stand, which costs seven dollars to start (so he would not have enough capital under the current system, since each child would only get five dollars). So, while distributing the capital evenly appears to be most fair, it forces the family to miss out on a valuable investment opportunity. The mother then has at least two choices: continue with the present course of action, or deviate in such a way that she can ensure that the family takes advantage of the financial opportunities provided via the purchase of a lemonade stand.

One immediate solution that comes to mind would be to give the older sibling the seven dollars she needs to start the stand, and giving only three dollars to the younger sibling. The hope is that when the older sibling starts the lemonade stand, she will then give her little brother a job and allow him to benefit from the additional resources. If all children contribute a percentage of their income to the family fund, then the older child will pay more in taxes and the family is going to win.

Assume that the older sister starts the lemonade stand with the seven dollars and earns total revenue in her first week of $14 dollars. Half of the $14 dollars is pure profit, so the family has created $7 dollars where it previously did not exist. The family is now better off financially, since everyone now has access to $17 dollars (the original $10 dollars, plus the seven dollar profit). But the progress may have been at the expense of family stability, because the older sibling may feel she has full rights to any profits earned on the lemonade stand. This leads to one sibling having $14 dollars, plus ownership in a long-term, profitable business venture, while the other sibling may have spent the three dollars given to him by the government (the mother). What's worse, the older sibling may choose to hire children down the street as employees, given that they are willing to work for a lower wage than her little brother.

A fairer solution to the family's financial dilemma would involve some degree of mild parental intervention. The truth of the matter is that the $10 dollars in the pot belongs to the entire family, with everyone having rights to an equal stake in the funds. It is also critical to remember that beyond maximizing revenue, the mother's job is to keep the family together. The mother could give seven dollars to the older sibling with the requirement that she hire her little brother to work with her on the lemonade stand. To push things further, she might ask that the older sibling contribute a percentage of her profits to the family fund (taxation), with the profits to be distributed among the children in an equitable fashion. She could then support the lemonade stand of the older sibling by providing incentives for the younger sibling to make purchases from the stand, rather than going to the lemonade stand down the street. This allows for a balanced distribution of wealth, as well as all the benefits that come from a capitalist society.

Trickle-down economics can work in this scenario, but it doesn't work because the older sibling *chooses* to share with her little brother. It works because the mother *forced* her do it. In the end, both children are happy and don't fight nearly as much as they would have otherwise.

This analogy can be expanded to an entire society. If the rich are allowed to benefit from Reaganomics and unfettered capitalism without sufficient government oversight, the stability of our society is ultimately at risk. The rich get richer and the poor get pissed off. The only solution in the end is anarchy, which doesn't benefit the society. This is the reason that some element of socialism is a necessary component in a strong capitalist society. The rich and the poor both benefit when there is balance and human compassion served on the plate of economic prosperity.

As of late, the irresponsible spending habits of the American people have been multiplied by our government. These choices included signing international trade agreements that opened markets to allow the rich to get richer, and for American workers to be left behind. Additionally, irresponsibility in government regulation and anti-trust efforts have left the middle class to fend for themselves in the advent of globalization. African-Americans have felt the worst of this, as the loss of high paying jobs has hit our community hard. As the old saying goes, "When the rest of America gets a cold, the black community catches pneumonia."

Gary, Indiana and Milwaukee, Wisconsin are two examples of manufacturing towns that have been destroyed since companies have found that their products can be made much more cheaply in China. Detroit, Gary and Milwaukee are grand examples of what happens when low skill jobs leave the country. Crime rises, as the school systems fail to provide adequate education during a period in which education is more important than ever. Kwame Kilpatrick was the mayor in Detroit during a tough economic period for the city. Mayor Kilpatrick, known as "The Hip Hop Mayor", happened to be the youngest, hippest and coolest mayor to ever run a major city. However, Kilpatrick fell as fast as he rose, getting caught up in one scandal after another, to the point of serious embarrassment. When I saw the rise and fall of Mayor Kilpatrick, I felt sorry for him.

I don't excuse his flamboyant behavior in office, but the truth of the matter is that most politicians misbehave in some way. Bill Clinton was a dirty old man with a list of sex stories that could fill an encyclopedia. There is an even longer list of conservative politicians who've been caught up in prostitution rings, extramarital affairs and even homosexual relationships. Again, not to excuse the behavior of Kilpatrick, but at the very least, I can say that he was a man who took on a job that most of us would not want. Detroit is a city with a mile of problems and 10 inches of resources. I wouldn't be mayor of Detroit for any amount of money in this world.

The destruction of cities and urban centers over the past decade creates a unique and interesting set of serious economic problems for the Hip Hop generation. These young people are tempted, as we all are, to follow in the footsteps of their parents, some of whom never chose to get a college education. While I am certainly a fan of education, I am not one to condemn those who choose not to get a college degree. The problem is that the myopic tradeoff between higher education and fast money has become more costly than ever.

There was a time when a high school graduate could get a high paid, low skilled factory job at The Ford Motor Company earning a wage that would have made many college graduates jealous. The wage would be strong enough that the individual could marry another worker in the same factory, raise children, save for a nice home and retire comfortably, assuming that the couple has engaged in responsible financial management. The workers could even send their children to college with the wages earned from their jobs at the factory.

Today, these jobs are few and far between. They've been replaced by jobs earning close to minimum wage, not enough money to live in this society. There are no benefits that come with these jobs, and certainly no retirement plan. The decision to pass up on education dooms many individuals to a life of poverty. Even those with college degrees sometimes find themselves at the short end of the economic stick. Middle management jobs are sometimes the first to disappear in exchange for high skilled, low priced labor which resides in India.

We must talk to our children about the value of education if we are going to find financial prosperity. Education is the difference in America between the rich and the poor and it is one of the commodities kept out of the hands of African-Americans for the past several hundred years. Now it is available in large quantities and much of my work in the black community is to convince our youth that education is the best way for us to survive during the next 30 years, as America's reign of financial dominance comes to a close.

Chapter 11

What are we going to do with our kids?

I talk to kids in the inner city on a regular basis about the joys of going to college. I feel sorry for the kids who miss out on the fun of college and the amazing opportunities that come with a college education. As a man who never enjoyed school as a child, I can explain that putting in the work when you are young will pay off for the rest of your life.

Some of the kids get the message, some of them do not. I don't get angry at those who don't listen, since young people have a natural tendency to want to do their own thing. People say kids in the inner city have bad outcomes because they are lazy. This couldn't be further from the truth. Kids in poverty actually work much harder than individuals I meet in the suburbs, because they know that hard work is the only way to get the things they need. So, the teenager who is willing to go to McDonald's and work a 10-hour shift every day baffles me. I sit and wonder if this kid truly understands that by working just five hours a day on a college campus, he can give himself financial rewards that last a lifetime.

What is saddest about the fact that so many youth are not choosing education is that there has never been a time in which education has become more critical. There are few opportunities for those who choose not to go to college, so this implies that education is clearly, without question, the final dividing line between the haves and have-nots. It is what makes the difference between a life of dreams and a life of drama. America is not a perfect country, but one great thing about America is that education is the expressway out of the land of poverty. I only hope that African-American children are willing to get in the car.

I don't always know exactly where to look to solve the problems of our youth. Of course you must start by looking at our personal choices, for most of our outcomes begin and end with individual decisions and how we react to our consequences. Our youth today are certainly different from their parents, but the truth is that this is the case for every generation throughout history. Young people are social deviants by definition, so you will never have any generation that runs in lockstep with the generation before. But the Hip Hop generation has certainly been raised in an era of instant gratification, which has played a role in the rise in the number of cases of Attention Deficit Disorder and flat out laziness. On that, Bill Cosby and I are likely to agree.

Another area where Mr. Cosby and I would both look is toward the parents. Some parents are not willing to do the right thing with their children and some parents are clearly better than others. I also agree that the message of the parent can overwhelm nearly every other message presented in society. My father (who was not the same as my sperm donor) taught me to be strong and focused. My mother taught me to be maniacally persistent. My parents shaped and molded me into the man that I am today.

What bothers me about looking only to parents for solutions is that it implies that poor parenting is the cause of most problems in the black community. There is variation in the quality of black parenting, the same way there is variation in the quality of white, Asian, Indian and Latino parenting. I have never once believed that black families have a monopoly on bad parenting, since I see good and bad parents of all ethnicities. So, the idea that black parents and the laziness of black youth are the primary causes of their economic condition is not only one that is laced with stereotypes, it is also an irresponsible morphing of the truth that allows the rest of America to feel vindicated in their treatment toward African-Americans. If I truly believe you are lazy and worthless, then I always have an excuse to discriminate against you.

I am also not a fan of the idea that black fathers not being in the home is the reason for racial inequality. It is nonsensical to blame a 400-year-old problem on a short-lived social phenomenon. Also, when one includes the income that comes via child support systems, the fact is that the economic impact is not as great as one might think. Finally, when Bill O'Reilly and others are tempted to ask me judgmental questions about the number of black single parents, I am equally quick to ask judgmental questions about the white parental divorce rate. Given that most white families also disrupt their relationships via divorce, one cannot place judgment on those who choose not to get married in the first place. At least having one parent implies that you are going to have stability. Also, having one parent in the home does not mean that there are no male role models. The swiftness with which some Americans are quick to place themselves in a position of moral superiority is a constant reminder of the impact of Jim Crow and racism.

One cannot deny that there is a dearth of black male role models, partly due to the prison systems in America. I will discuss the prison system in more detail later in the book, but the United Nations and other organizations have expressed serious concern about the United States prison systems and the fact that the human rights of African-Americans are not respected in our society. Like the Jews during the holocaust, we have a society that has been persuaded that it is okay to destroy black families because black men are "bad people." Had the Nazis not persuaded the masses that the Jews were inferior (via propaganda and other mind control mechanisms), the "final solution" would not have been deemed nearly as acceptable.

Would better parenting help solve problems in the black community? Absolutely, seeing as good parenting can be quite powerful. But one can always say that a child's life would be perfect if his parents were perfect. Almost any limitation can be overcome in the presence of perfect behavior. But the expectation that we are going to suddenly breed a generation of 36 million "super negroes" who can overcome all social limitations with a single bound is a bit ridiculous. Like American corporations, individual behavior ultimately responds to the incentives that have been put in place by the structural mechanisms of the world in which the individual exists. Any economics textbook will explain this in detail.

The fact that we have created a world in which African-American youth are vilified for not being mistake free should concern us all. We must also remember that in addition to the impact of the parent, there is a whole world surrounding the individual that is going to have an influence as well.

After one focuses on the individual and his or her parents, one must then turn to the school system. As I've continuously stated, money matters in America. It is clear that inner city schools do not have the same resources as the schools in the suburbs. As a result of this economic disparity, these schools are going to consistently struggle to get what they need. It is difficult in this country to find ways to educate children properly when our schools don't

129

have the necessary books, teachers and other tools to provide a proper education.

I speak at a lot of schools every year. I grow weary of seeing schools in the city struggling to obtain the basic necessities. There are long lists of problems and a short stack of teachers who are getting tired of solving those problems. I don't blame teachers for not being able to do the job. I blame a system that would rather declare war on imaginary terrorists than to declare war on a school system in disrepair. When I leave the city and visit the suburbs, the clouds in the sky seem to disappear, the streets get cleaner and the birds chirp a little louder. Suddenly, going to school is no longer frightening, it is fulfilling. Teachers and counselors are no longer obstacles to learning, but vehicles to enlightenment. There are plenty of books, the sports teams have nicer uniforms, and college prep programs are being created left and right. It's a completely different world.

What is also sad is that there are cases in which the attitudes of the individuals associated with the institution match the state of the institution itself. Our inner city schools are nothing more than a modern overseer system, similar to penitentiaries. Individuals responsible for monitoring those who come through the system do not share a similar background with those they are monitoring, and do not live in the same communities.

I recall giving a speech at a middle school in New York that was 90% black and Hispanic. Like many other inner city schools in America, black boys were put in special education at horrific rates, and there was little effort to challenge a system that was condemning young black geniuses to a life of destructive self-fulfilling prophecies. When I was asked what I thought about the appearance of the building upon entering, I honestly stated that it reminded me of a cross between a prison and an insane asylum. This is how our precious black children are being educated.

But I give the teachers at this school tremendous credit. The six teachers for the 7th grade class, all white females from the suburbs, sat with me at a table to ask my opinion on what they could do to reach their black and Latino boys. One of them stated to me, quite plainly, "Dr. Watkins, in case you haven't noticed, we're all white females."

"I hadn't really noticed, but thanks for telling me," I stated in jest.

The teachers expressed concern over the alarming failure rates of their black and Latino boys. They expressed even more frustration over the fact that the school system did not seem to be in a rush to get black male teachers into the classroom. The original plan for my speech was that I would address the "promising students": the ones they'd tagged for higher education and greater success in life. Instead, I requested just the opposite: I wanted the worst of the worst.

I went into the Special Education class, the one for students who'd been labeled as having behavioral problems and learning disorders. I wanted to talk to these youth because I was one of them. As a child, I too was told that I had behavioral and learning disorders and that I was not college material. So, I knew that at least 10% of these kids were likely geniuses, and another 50% of them were of average intelligence. Perhaps there were a few who had true learning disabilities, but the reality was that the system evaluating them was far more flawed than the individuals they claimed to be evaluating.

131

I talked to the kids for an hour about the value of education and going to college. They paid close attention, like I had an Xbox video game coming out of my face. Their teacher, a white male, was shocked that I could keep their attention for the entire hour. He stated afterward that he'd had 20 guest speakers throughout the year and none of them had been able to maintain the attention of these students for the entire time. I simply explained to the man that these kids were basically my cousins and I knew how to deal with them. We need teachers in black school systems who know how to deal with black children. That doesn't mean the teachers need to be black, but they must have some additional training to deal with black youth.

I saw some random "expert" on a "60 Minutes" segment discussing the state of the education system. The man was attempting to argue that more resources won't make a difference in the quality of our schools. He went on to argue that many of the pathetic schools in the inner city are run by blacks, implying that not only do African-Americans not care about their own youth, they are shiftless buffoons when it comes to money management. I've heard similar arguments from members of oppressive groups around the world, as oppressor attitudes are shockingly consistent and universal. A friend of mine from India once explained to me that additional government resources being allocated to create opportunities for "the untouchables" were a waste of time, in large part due to the fact that the people were too lazy to efficiently use these opportunities.

Stereotypes against historically oppressed groups are quite common, as the world has been trained to believe that when it comes to managing money, white men are gods and black people are idiots. But when it comes to

132

poor money management, few institutions are worse than the Pentagon which has been known to spend $500 for a toilet seat. They also fail to look to the airline and automobile industries, the ultimate welfare queens of American capitalism. These industries consistently seek government bailouts in the form of tariffs and subsidies. I won't begin to discuss the Financial Crisis of 2008 – 2009, as we saw our entire global financial system artificially inflated and subsequently destroyed by individuals who are not black. Rather, people are usually quick to point to black administrators in inner city schools and historically black colleges and universities as the most wasteful individuals in American education and industry.

My response to any individual who attempts to argue that additional resources would not solve the education problem is this: prove it. Create a mandate that all schools receive equal funding, no matter where they are located, and then see what happens. Such a law would surely see a dramatic increase in graduation rates and improvements in the educational outcomes of students. Money is the key to salvation in a capitalist society. Until the funds and resources are equivalent, then all conversations about parenting, culture and individual responsibility are absolutely and unconditionally moot. Another barrier to progress in many school systems can be guidance counselors. I couldn't help but notice that guidance counselors in inner city schools are far less likely to suggest college as an option than counselors at schools in the suburbs. I am not sure why this is the case, seeing as I teach a lot of idiots who come out of the suburbs. This is not to say that all of my students are idiots, but some of them spend more time in a beer bottle than a text book. What is incredibly sad about this is that if they'd gone through one of our horrible inner city schools, they would have ended up not going to college at all. Instead, they grew up in environments where college was the rule and not the exception. They were encouraged to pursue education by their guidance counselors and not discouraged by them.

In fact, I feel that high school guidance counselors have more power than they should. The idea that you can analyze someone for a couple of years at the age of 16 and make (what you think is) an accurate prediction of what they are capable of for the rest of their life is absolutely ridiculous. I have changed dramatically since I was 16, and if I had accepted the labels placed upon me at that time, those labels would have formed a self-fulfilling prophecy leading me to a life of misery and mediocrity.

When I speak with youth either in person or via email, I start off with the assumption that all black kids should go to college. If George Bush can graduate from the top university in the nation, then every black kid in America can go to college somewhere. The truth is that the default educational choice should start from the top, not the bottom. We should assume each child can go to college and speak to him/her as if college is the expectation, not the exception. Going to high school is an expectation now, but it was the exception at one point in time. It was due to higher standards that we eventually witnessed stronger community performance. We must demand and expect the most from our children, because their economic futures are highly dependent on their decision to become educated.

Chapter 12

Teaching Ownership to our children

Why this is the guide to wealth and social freedom in America

One of the most common misperceptions about wealth is the perceived correlation between wealth and high income. Many Americans make this mistake on a regular basis, as they presume that the individual with the highest salary is the one in the best long-term financial situation. Many black doctors, lawyers and professors are the absolute worst when it comes to understanding that high income is no guarantee that you are actually wealthy. In fact, a high income can fool you into thinking you're doing okay when you're really not.

There is an old saying that says, "if you give a man a fish, you feed him for a day. If you teach him how to fish, you feed him for a lifetime." That statement is silly. The truth of the matter is that both the person giving away the fish and the one who is receiving the gift are missing the game entirely. The person who is really getting rich is the guy who owns the land that the pond is on, who is renting the land out to fishing teachers and their students.

In America, wealth is all about ownership.

NBA players think in terms of income, when the team owners are the ones who truly possess real wealth. Rappers "bling" and "ball" out of control when they receive their royalty checks, even though the recording label is

135

going to replace him with another kid from the projects the following year. Many doctors and lawyers feel that they are on top of the world with their six-figure salaries and luxury cars (with high car notes to boot). The truth is that many of them would be destitute if they were to incur a sudden job loss. In fact, many of these high-paid professionals go into so much debt that they die owing money.   In other words, they become high paid sharecroppers, who never truly own a piece of the American dream.

This may surprise you, but the greatest models in black America for proving the value of ownership are rappers and the Nation of Islam. Don't get me wrong. Many rappers are either broke or close to it. But there are some rappers who can't get a record deal and become shining examples of the old saying, "necessity is the mother of invention."

I once met a highly enterprising rapper in the Midwest. To protect his privacy, I will call him Mr. Anonymous. I met Mr. Anonymous while appearing on a show with him to discuss the value of education. I enjoyed my visit primarily because of his hospitality. He and I are both fans of hip hop and this connection opened the door to a more significant and meaningful dialogue. But when it came to our comparative knowledge of hip hop music, he was the teacher and I was the student.

Mr. Anonymous has a solid recording style, but is an older hip hop artist, probably in his mid to late thirties. Despite his age, Mr. Anonymous has a tremendous flow, professionalism and conscientiousness about his music that is quite impressive.
In his work, Mr. Anonymous sought to specifically counter some of the dominant artists in hip hop; those whom he feels conduct modern-day minstrel shows. While hip hop

is certainly a diverse art from, there is certainly merit to his argument. The idea of corporate executives pushing artists to be more "thug-like" is problematic, as it encourages behavior that matches preconceived stereotypes of black men. I am a fan of Lil Wayne's work, but I am not a fan of Wayne's life, which is full of drugs, guns and random women. Honestly, men like that don't live past the age of 40, I hope he is different.

My friend Mr. Anonymous had not, the last I checked, received a record deal. We all know that many record labels are hesitant to sign conscious, intelligent artists, since these individuals don't sell as well as Lil Wayne and other rappers willing to say anything on a record. One can't blame the record labels for not signing artists like Mr. Anonymous, because the individuals running the labels have very little incentive to sign any artist who is not going to maximize corporate profitability. Additionally, they see almost no financial value in a conscientious artist. Conscientious black music does nothing for the executive's bottom line, his life or his community. I am not sure why we would expect anyone in any other community to feel compelled to do anything that will help black people. The problem is that many whites expect African-Americans to sit peacefully at the American table, yet those in power are unwilling to right the wrongs that lead to financial and cultural dominance being exerted upon people of color. You can't have it both ways. If negative hip hop is being distributed by white owned corporations and hurting the black community, then we must be intelligent when considering where to focus our outrage.

Mr. Anonymous didn't allow the lack of a record deal slow him down. He made his own CD, which was strong and professional. He then went on to sell his music at parties, out of the trunk of his car, and to anyone who would listen to it. He sold the CDs for $10 dollars each and spent a lot of time learning the fundamentals of business: production, finance, marketing and distribution.

In terms of production, he learned the value of creating a quality product. He knew that his work had to be as hot as the best artists in America, and he fully understood that one doesn't need the backing of a record label in order to make good music. He received cheap studio time from a friend who leased the space to local artists in the area and he eventually invested in creating his own studio from home. He was thus able to create a quality product in a reasonably short amount of time.

At that point, Mr. Anonymous would ensure that the packaging of the product was solid and professional. He found a company that could put a flashy label on the front of his CDs, and he then found the right images to put inside the CD jacket. This led to him obtaining an understanding of Photoshop, lighting, photography and CD creation to help him create the final package.

After creating the first version of the CD, he would then send the CD to a duplication company to have his first 1,000 copies made. Each copy cost him $1 to make. If he didn't have the capital to put up $1,000 for the first 1,000 copies, he would lower the initial investment in production by creating CDs "on the fly": Copying, stamping and labeling the CDs from home. It cost him a little more per CD to produce, but this allowed him to avoid the cost of producing a large number of CDs for initial inventory. Having a lack of capital helped Mr. Anonymous learn the value of good cash management for his business.

After Mr. Anonymous received his first batch of CDs, he would then begin banging the pavement to market and distribute his product. He used the Internet and a savvy web marketing strategy that included both viral marketing through social networking sites, as well as some degree of paid advertising. He also used avenues such as Youtube.com to shoot and distribute videos. One of his "homeboys" was an expert at Search Engine Optimization, so he was able to secure the proper tags for his videos to ensure that everyone had a chance to see him in action. The videos did not receive the same distribution they would have gotten through a major record label, but it certainly provided Mr. Anonymous with some "heat" behind his product. Some of his videos would be viewed by as many as 50,000 people, leading them to visit his website, providing him with additional brand recognition.

Additionally, Mr. Anonymous was able to sell CDs out of his car to those in the community who came to know his name. Tying his music to a message of educational empowerment led to additional speaking opportunities and other options. These events allowed him to sell his CDs and, in some cases, collect a speaking fee. By producing, marketing, distributing and financing his own product, he was able to achieve a profit margin roughly 40 times greater than artists who sign with major labels. Each release would sell about 10,000 copies once Mr. Anonymous achieved name brand recognition. The profit margin he earned on record sales was equivalent to a traditional artist selling 400,000 copies, since he was able to keep all the money from the sale of his recordings.

There were additional benefits to the fact that Mr. Anonymous owned his own venture. I will list some of these advantages below:

1) He would never be released from his label

I make fun of the rapper Sean "P Diddy" Combs quite a bit. Honestly, he hasn't made good music since the rapper "The Notorious B.I.G." was alive. I can't lie about that. But one thing I also can't lie about is the fact that Diddy controls his own destiny. He runs an enterprise, a powerful empire that makes major deals that change the world. I respect Diddy for the way he runs his organization, even though I was disappointed with his role in the East Coast/West Coast conflict that led to the murders of Tupac Shakur and The Notorious B.I.G.

Diddy and Mr. Anonymous prove one clear point: when you run the show, you are liberated. Another good example is the rapper TI and his label, Grand Hustle Records. While TI has had trouble with the law, I perceive him to be an intelligent businessman. When you decide how your bottom line is going to be structured, you decide what products are going to be pushed and promoted. You also decide which ventures are going to receive the greatest financial support. Now that's power!

When I became a public scholar, I noticed that many of my predecessors had a simple model for getting their ideas to the public:

Find a speakers bureau, typically one controlled by whites.
Find a publisher, again controlled by whites.
Get a publicist to help you access the media, again signing with another white person.

Next step: Appear in the media as much as possible, typically controlled by whites.

Gain a large platform of financial success, book deals, speaking engagements, corporate sponsorship, and tremendous visibility, again controlled by whites. The lights shine brightly upon you, but you have no say about when the lights turn dim.

How depressing.

First off, I remind you that I have no problem with white people, but I do think that dependence upon whites is not good for the African American community. Racism is still a serious problem, and we are not doing ourselves any favors by depending upon those who've been trained to oppress us. I recall an interesting conversation I had with a prominent black radio show host. She'd worked in media for a number of years and with a lot of major networks. When describing her experience with the speaker bureaus, the woman sighed and said to me, "They just wanna sign the hot new nigger on TV."

I took her words to heart, seeing as I never knew how long I would be the "hot new nigger on TV." Like rap artists, public scholars get used and dragged through the "rags to riches and back to rags" mill as well. I never wanted to be one of those people. The destination doesn't matter to me nearly as much as my ability to decide what that destination is going to be. I would rather have a bicycle that is mine, than a jet plane that belongs to someone else. Both of them can travel the same distance across America if you peddle long enough.

So, I worked with my brother, who helped me invest the capital necessary to found Great black Speakers, LLC, our black speaker's bureau. Within one year, my brother had 250 African-American speakers under his label, and he treated them all with decency and integrity. I'd worked with other bureaus, both white and black, and it bothered me that there are many (again, both black and white) who regularly profit from the dreams of others. One bureau I dealt with took on all speakers for a fee (with the fee being paid by the speaker) and then did nothing to promote the individual for speaking opportunities. This was sad, pathetic and hurtful.

My brother and I applied the speaker bureau model to start a publicity firm and publishing company as well. We were a welcome site for all those in the black community who wanted to have a voice, but didn't quite know how to express it. It wasn't easy, and the success was not nearly as immediate as it would have been had I signed with a larger, more established bureau. However, there was an asset in this process that you can't put a price on. That asset was freedom: The freedom to work hard without the fear of a pink slip. The freedom of knowing that someone isn't going to call you and tell you that your books are "too black," your speeches too radical or your public image unfit for the vision they have for you. It was the freedom to be an honest and truthful intellectual in the public sphere. That was the greatest profit of all.

Mr. Anonymous, whom I discussed above, also knew what freedom feels like. He knew that he would never lose faith in his music or drop himself from his label. This allowed him to sleep at night, even if the money was not as big as it can be for some fly-by-night entertainers.

2) Mr. Anonymous could also make music that fit his taste, without someone telling him what to release.

Whites and blacks see the world differently. What we see as necessary and fundamental to the advancement of equality, some whites see as political nonsense. I was shocked to find out about some who characterized my discussions on race as being too political. They would say that "my politics" would make it tough for me to be hired at other universities. There were those on my own campus who stated that my politics were too radical to be affiliated with my own university's initiatives to help inner city black children. It's quite disturbing when a predominantly white university feels that it is better equipped to prepare black youth for college than a well-known black professor who motivates black youth for a living. Such ideologies are reminders of the paternalistic overseer mentality held by many American institutions: black people are pawns of the institution, while white males control the institutions. This is the case in our school systems, the prison system and other systems throughout America, and stands as yet another reminder that we were formerly a country that owned black slaves.

What has always bothered me the most about having a heartfelt public discussion on equality reduced to mere politics is that I have never discussed these issues as part of a broader political game. I have never once wanted to be a congressman, councilman, dean, college president or high ranking university

143

administrator. I knew that a man with my ideas and the willingness to express them would never be rewarded by the establishment for doing so. I do what I do because my actions reflect the core beliefs which lie at the bottom of my heart. Political jockeying is something I've never tried to master, and I would probably not be very good at it anyway.

These ideas relate to the experience of Mr. Anonymous (the rapper above) because his decision to control and run his own small enterprise created within him the ability to make music that fit his soul and god-given purpose. He wanted to help the community with his music, and he never has to worry about someone telling him that his life's work was politically incorrect.

Alicia Keys, a powerful singer, went through a major controversy when she stated her personal theory that gangster rap was a tool for the government to get black people to kill one another. While I am stretched to agree with her theory, I applaud her willingness to make statements that are both heartfelt and capable of opening the door to further discussion.

When Kanye West said "George Bush doesn't care about black people", I agreed with him 100%. George Bush didn't seem to care about black people. But the fact is that making a statement that was deemed wasteful and unnecessary by his record label surely led to some sweaty palms that day. Had Kanye been the person in control of his own label, he would have considered his sociopolitical stance to be a necessary cost of doing business.

The concept of independence applies for any corporation that closed its doors on September 12,

2001, out of respect for the victims of the terror attacks the day before. The truth is that he who has the gold makes the rules, and individuals in control of the business enterprise get to decide which losses are meaningful and which are wasteful. Most white corporations are not going to be happy about losing money for the sake of the black community, because African-Americans are not the ones paying the bills.

3) Mr. Anonymous controlled the rate at which his music was being produced and promoted.

Mr. Anonymous, by running his own label, didn't have to worry about being "shelved" as many artists are in hip hop. The same is true in publishing and any other industry. The truth is that whether it is television, music, media or publishing, there is almost always far more available talent than opportunities for that talent to display itself. The "highly paid celebrity bus" has 30 seats and 3,000 people are qualified to get a ticket.

"Getting signed" doesn't lead to the riches that most artists expect. I have met literally thousands of young authors, rappers, speakers, and TV personalities who all have the same dream of getting signed by a record label. Some of them are already signed by a company promising to promote and distribute their images and products to the world. I feel sorry for many of these wannabe celebrities for at least two reasons: First, they think that sending me their book, CD or other product is going to lead to my picking up the phone and making a magical phone call that will make them instantly famous. It's not that I don't care about their work; it's that I don't have that magic phone number. People think that because they saw you on TV, you must

145

obviously control the world. This is far from the truth, as many celebrities get pimped like everyone else.

Secondly, the up and coming artists don't realize that the chances of being signed by a label, network or publisher are few and far between. While we are quick to ridicule high school basketball players with hoop dreams of going to the NBA, the reality is that there are a lot of adults with hoop dreams of being the next Oprah Winfrey, Tom Joyner or Toni Morrison. I don't enjoy squashing the dreams of anyone, but I try to help the individual keep their understanding of the situation both realistic and achievable. I certainly believe that the highest heights of success can be reached, but the likelihood of success is, in my opinion, lower when you use standard and uncreative approaches. I let the budding star know that while I believe it to be critical that they continue sending query letters to agents and doing auditions for radio shows, they should try to replicate the patterns of Kanye West or Mr. Anonymous and find their own voice. In many cases, opportunities are not given, they are created.

More specifically, I encourage newbie media types to use the Internet as their pathway to getting their voice heard. While the web does not provide the same audience as a strong TV or radio show, the beautiful thing is that it provides instant worldwide distribution. I have seen people start off with nothing to create a daily audience of over 10,000 readers, viewers and listeners. Additionally, building an audience online serves as a proving and polishing ground for those who want to eventually hit mainstream media outlets. For example, "Buck Hollywood," a very entertaining online show, gets hundreds of thousands of viewers each week. In some ways, you can analogize building an online audience to waiting for a bus, but walking toward your destination until the bus arrives. Either way, you get the fulfillment of knowing that you are moving closer to your destination with each step.

The third reason I feel bad for the authors and speakers with "hoop dreams" is that their image of what it means to "be signed" is somewhat skewed. The reality is that a label can sign you, control all the rights to your image and enslave you without giving you very much compensation at all. An individual who does not understand business models stands as clear prey to those who run major organizations.

The group New Edition is a perfect example of corporate exploitation within entertainment. After winning a local music competition, the kids from the projects of Boston were signed to a record deal. Their first album resulted in several number one hits and a whirlwind tour that took them around the world. Upon returning home, the teens thought their hard work would pay off with a big check for each of them that would allow their families to live happily ever after. How much money did they receive on that first check? $1.87.

After taking out all the expenses of the tour, and everyone else getting their cut of the investment, the group received almost nothing. This was in spite of becoming a household name and having several songs that were in the regular radio rotation at stations around the world. The group was not released from the contract until after the year 2000. At this point, they were grown men with their best years behind them.

I have seen other artists "get signed" to find out that they wished they hadn't. The truth is that getting

147

signed is not all it's cracked up to be, and it is important to obtain the economic knowledge necessary to keep others from stealing your dreams. Models of great independent success are individuals like E-40, who wrote a song "They'll find a new nigger next year" to describe what happens to artists who sign with major labels.

4) Mr. Anonymous educated himself a great deal about business and industry.

By being educated on the production and distribution process, Mr. Anonymous was not wowed or cheated by any old record label executive who came his way. He didn't perceive a record deal to be his path to fame and fortune. He fully understood the pitfalls and constraints of being an artist and could pick and choose among potential suitors once the record labels came along to try to work with him.

I encourage anyone who wants to do anything in any field to spend some time studying business. One of the consequences of living in a capitalist society is that most industries have a business model. Most of these models need financial fuel to keep them going. You must be able to interpret and understand business to know where this financial fuel is coming from, and how you can control it.

A college student majoring in business, who attempts to become a filmmaker, is far more likely to get a foot in the door than someone who simply shows up to one audition after another trying to get their big break. The business major can speak the language of the studio, describe what investors are looking for in terms of marketability, and even promote and distribute their own projects if necessary.

The example is no different from two men trying to get a woman to have sex with them. The man with the most sisters, who has spent time studying women, listening to them and knowing what they want is likely to get the most sexual opportunities. My own luck with women shows quite clearly that I don't have enough sisters!

By studying business models in this way, Mr. Anonymous effectively gave himself an education that was far better than that of any business school. Rather than learning theories and ideas, he was able to learn concepts on the job and apply them. There is no better place to be educated than the university of life. Although Mr. Anonymous never earned any advanced degrees, speaking to him made me feel as though I was talking to another professor.

5) Mr. Anonymous was not forced to take the first record deal that came along.

Because Mr. Anonymous found his own way to the "financial faucet," he realized a couple of things about himself: First, he learned that he didn't need to make millions to feel good about making music. Secondly, he figured out that he only needed to make a decent living in order to be happy. Not that making millions wouldn't be fun, but he wouldn't accept millions of dollars in exchange for the creative freedom and empowerment that came from doing work that inspired his community. So, when his name grew and the major labels came along to try to sign him, Mr. Anonymous declined all of the offers. He realized that he was already making enough money with his own system that he would actually end up earning less money, with less stability if he were to sign with one of the large record labels.

He had achieved true independence.

Mr. Anonymous reminds me of why we must be careful about elitism in the black community. The educated African-American may feel that he/she has greater control and self-determination because he's been invited into the great white institutions of America. It is tempting to believe that the artist, writer, or actor with crossover appeal has achieved the American dream and possesses the power that appears to come with it. But what is most critical is to remember the importance of black institution building. These are institutions of wealth, empowerment and ultimately liberation that take a long time to create. It may be easier to simply jump on the backs of previously established institutions and ride those opportunities into the sunset. But the greater challenge is that such institutions don't provide you with the ability to draw up the blueprints to your own set of outcomes.

You can analogize institution building to growing a tree. Trees that have been growing for years are going to be taller, with thicker, sturdier branches. They are the ones most likely to survive and have the greatest ability to fight for valuable oxygen, water and sunlight. While others have climbed the tall, previously established economic and institutional trees and staked out their positions, there is still room to grab a branch of someone else's tree and call it your own. But the truth is that it would still someone else's tree and you don't even own the thick, strong branch on which you stand.

There is something to be said about coming into the forest with a pocket full of seeds and planting trees for yourself and those you love. The small trees are going to fight for sunlight, but with hard work and nurturing, the little tree can survive. Eventually, the little tree grows stronger and can live on its own. Although it is still tiny next to the big sycamores that have lived for hundreds of years, your tree is still your source of pride. You OWN that tree. While others peer down upon you from their tall and sturdy branches, some of these individuals look down on you with envy. They know that although their branches are strong and high in the sky, someone can take their branch away at any second. They also realize they have no control over the direction of the tree, and they will not be able to leave the tree to their children when they die, as someone else will simply be given the branch upon which they've been perched.

So, while others may make fun of you for planting your own tree of entrepreneurship and question why you fight for sunlight, I encourage you to ignore their negative words. You should always realize that deep down; your little tree is going to be your source of liberation in a capitalist society. Go plant an entrepreneurship tree right now.

Chapter 13

How Money Can Destroy Families

I am a veteran of the Child Support system. I am not just a vet, but a hardened one. I only created one child, but I have paid quite a bit of money over the years to provide financial support for my child. I don't regret paying so much in child support, because that was my obligation as a father. I believe strongly in having an empowered Child Support system, and it bothers me when individuals do not live up to their responsibilities.

In addition to paying child support for my own daughter, I dealt with the consequences of other men and their bad decisions. I was in a long-term relationship with a woman whose son was not receiving support from his father. Therefore, many of the financial expectations fell on me, which I didn't mind one bit. I also have several godchildren whose fathers have chosen not to support their children financially. I don't mind taking up that slack as well.

It was not my decision to spend the first 18 years of my child's life paying child support. I would have much rather been her father, right there in the home. I loved her mother dearly and thought she was the most beautiful woman on earth. She was my first girlfriend and the love I had was deep, strong and loyal.

But we were from different sides of the tracks, which made it difficult to continue the relationship when I decided to change my life and get an education. I moved to a nearby town to go to college and I presume that my talk of education, college and the future made me sound like a wet blanket. I was certainly no fun as an 18-year-old, that's for sure. My freshman year of college was spent thinking about the future and all the opportunities education could provide for our child. While most adults might consider this admirable, the truth was that I was a bit of a drag to my girlfriend.

My daughter's birth had nearly perfect timing; I wonder if she was aware of my class schedule while lying in the womb. She was born over Christmas break during my freshman year of college, so I was able to take my final exams and still be there for the birth of my first and only child. I didn't have a car to get back and forth to the hospital, so I just stayed at the hospital for three days. The hospital was kind enough to put a cot in my girlfriend's room so I could sleep beneath her as she endured the worst pain I'd ever seen in my life.

As we spent nearly 18 hours in labor waiting for our daughter to be born, I would pass the time reading the academic bulletin for my university. The bulletin contained descriptions of all the different majors available on the University of Kentucky campus. I would scheme and plot over all the academic possibilities, and how I could get a double or triple major with the highest GPA possible. I'd started my college career with a 4.0 grade point average, which gave me a lot of motivation. Because I'd never experienced this kind of academic success, I certainly wasn't going to give it up.

When my daughter was born, the feeling was amazing. She had a head full of hair, and looked as beautiful as the sun is bright. The next stage of my life was beginning, and I welcomed the future with open, yet hesitant arms. Money was certainly going to play a huge role in raising this child, but knowing that I would likely have a college degree in just three years gave me hope.

While I expected to raise my daughter as a family, things changed after my child was born. My talk of education and planning for the future apparently didn't sound as appealing as the words coming out of the mouths of other men and I soon found myself without the woman I loved. I would have done anything to keep her, even leave college. But when you are 18 years old, a lot of men talk a good game to get the attention of women. I am sure that the beauty of my daughter's mother brought on a new suitor every single day, and I can't say that I was the best of the pack at that time.

When my daughter's mother left me, I was absolutely devastated. After spending several days crying on the floor of my dorm room, I picked up my face and moved on with my life. I felt that one day, my hard work would pay off and my daughter's mother would be sorry that she let go of a man who was working hard to create a good future for his child.

The future brought what I expected, as my life took me to places I'd never imagined. On the other hand, I saw some things happen on the other side of the family that made me feel bad for those who chose not to make the right choices. But I never said "I told you so." I felt sorry for my close friends who chose not to educate themselves or plan for the future. I had to watch them experience the consequences we all must endure when we do not plan ahead. What was most painful was that I saw my own child being influenced by those who did not possess my educational values. The need to "keep it real" can sometimes be detrimental, because such a mindset does not always embody the best educational values. I like to "keep it real" myself, but I believe that "keeping it real" also means "keeping it educated." Unfortunately, much of urban America has a different mindset from my own.

I am a fan of the company "Dangerous Negro," which was founded by some black male graduate students who are close friends of my family. One of the students is a Harvard graduate, another is from Stanford University. Their approach to "keeping it real" is to redefine blackness in a way that is hip and productive. They explain that a "Dangerous Negro" is an educated individual who becomes a threat to the establishment by equipping himself/herself with the intellectual tools necessary to be successful. That's what greatness and blackness are all about. This is also the model I've worked to incorporate in my own life, using education as my weapon of choice.

The first 18 years of my daughter's life were difficult. I tried to be a father, volunteering myself to attend PTA meetings, or to do other things I thought fathers were supposed to do. But when it came to interacting with my child, I felt like an outsider. I didn't see my child as much as I wanted, I couldn't get custody of her, and I would even be accused by some members of her family of "acting white" when I would speak with proper English. I find that accusation ironic, given that I am often penalized by white America for being too black.

I often wondered if it were not for the substantial amounts of money I was sending every month, if I would have been invited to be part of my daughter's life at all. This bothered me a great deal and kept me up at night. I have seven godchildren and thousands of black youth I speak to every year. I honestly believe that, on a subconscious level, that part of the reason I spend so much time helping children is because I wanted to be allowed to help my own daughter. Being shut out of her life was incredibly frustrating, for we live in a world where the rights of the custodial parent can reign supreme.

I found that the Child Support courts were of no help in my quest to be a better parent. The tremendous effort put forth to collect money from me come hell or high water was not utilized to ensure that I had an opportunity to be involved in the life of my child. I learned a lot during this process, as I found out that many of the "dead-beat dads" in America are actually not dead-beats. Some so-called "dead-beats" (though not all of them) were created by the system.

This is not to say that I have a problem with the idea of paying child support. I grew up without my biological father taking care of his child support responsibility, so I have firsthand experience seeing the devastation that comes with the abandonment of children. I've also seen my goddaughters struggle, having children with men who are not as financially responsible as I'd like for them to be. The truth of the matter is that those who try to do the right thing end up subsidizing the behavior of those who do the wrong things.

But I have also found that individuals who endure the system are sometimes treated like criminals, even when they try to do the right thing. I have seen men lose their jobs and go to jail because they could not keep up their child support payments. The courts are quick to implement an order to increase child support, but are not nearly as eager to have the support reduced during tough economic times.

There is also the issue of accountability for child support funds. I never had a problem sending large sums of money for the support of my child. But I was disturbed when, in spite of the large amounts of money I was sending, my child did not appear to be getting what she needed. When I saw her living in a tiny apartment and sharing a room with her teenage brother at the age of 14, I was clearly bothered by this. In spite of my protest, anger, and disappointment, nothing was done in my favor.

So, I spent years sending money on behalf of a child who I felt was not receiving any meaningful percentage of the money that I was sending. It wasn't the amount of money that bothered me. What got to me was that I feel I could have given my daughter 100 times that value in love, life lessons and educational opportunity. I wanted to make her a product of me, but instead, she was a product of people who'd made little or no financial investment in her well-being. All I wanted was for her mother to say "You need to see your father," or "Listen to your father." Instead, I felt like an uncle: the outside option, or the person you only see if you feel like it. If I disciplined my child too much, she was simply allowed to hide behind her mother and not see me for months at a time. I've never thought that seeing your father should be an option given to an 8-year-old child. It should be mandatory. Eventually, my daughter would regularly decline the option to see me, as only God knows what people were saying about me when I wasn't around.

I respect the power of the mother. Without our mothers, most of us would be nothing. I also respect the need for children to have good fathers. What must also be respected is that beyond having a mother and/or father, children need LOVE. Love can come from many sources, and although we might make fun of families that have "play cousins," or seemingly broken constructs (i.e. the man who has two kids from a woman he never married, and another child with the woman he is dating right now), the truth of the matter is that the religious and social constraints we put on families are not always the method by which God communicates our ability to love one another.

While many Americans take a self-righteous attitude toward those who choose not to be married, the truth is that high divorce rates imply that most of us should never be married at all. But without judging the merits of marriage in this chapter, I will only say that my judgment of parents and children comes down to one question: is the child getting the love, nurturing and life lessons that he/she needs? If the answer is "yes," then I am fine with whatever family structure is used to raise the child. Finally, I also respect the reality that there should be structural incentives for families to stay together. Money matters in the entire incentive process. The same courts that are quick to go after fathers who don't pay their child support should be equally quick to ensure that these men are allowed to spend time with their children. Those mothers who use child support and child custody as weapons should be reminded that two people chose to create the child(ren) in question and no one individual should be allowed to dominate the relationship.

The government can, should and does play a role in whether or not families stay together. Tax laws have been changed to encourage Americans to get married. There are corporate programs to support family psychological health, physical health, and insurance coverage for all its members. There are laws designed to protect the millions of families broken up in the heat of divorce, so there should be equally strong protections for those who do not make the mistake of marrying someone they were not meant to marry. Throughout history, governments have always played a role in the structure of our lives, so the notion that one cannot and should not look toward the government for support in critical areas of our well-being is somewhat contradictory to every other dimension of our very existence.

When it comes to child support, I've seen men hide under the radar in order to avoid being incarcerated for not paying an amount they cannot afford. This pressure increases the incentive to pay absolutely nothing if you can't make the full amount, thus further alienating children from their parents. This approach should be exchanged for a system similar to that used for student loans. Because the government is committed to providing access to education and also wants students to repay their debts, there are many options for renegotiation as the student runs into financial problems. A student can get forbearance, deferment or even loan forgiveness in some cases. A system laced with compassion gives all parties a direct incentive to come to the negotiating table to work through their differences.

On the issue of child support, it seems logical that invoking a bit more compassion may also open the door for more effective collection on past due amounts. Individuals who are behind in their child support should be given options to catch up the arrears, have the amount adjusted for their income, and be given the same rights to parenthood as the custodial parent. Additionally, there should be accountability to ensure that child support funds are being used for items that directly or indirectly support the lifestyle of the child. Paying light bills, car notes and home mortgages are fine, but hair, nails and vacations are not. The system must invoke personal responsibility on both sides of the table, not just one.

When the custodial parent runs short on funds and can't maintain the pre-existing lifestyle they've established for their children, they are allowed to simply force their children to endure a lower standard of living. When the non-custodial parent suffers a job loss or reduction in income, he/she is still obligated to come up with a certain amount of money. You then have what effectively amounts to a debtor's prison when we incarcerate non-custodial parents for not being able to raise the money necessary to stay out of jail.

Black financial empowerment would also play a direct role in strengthening the family in other ways. The challenges of black men to find financial success in a racially biased society can determine whether or not these men choose to get married. Improperly educating black boys in our public schools reduces the likelihood that they will become suitable husbands and fathers in the future. Many are more likely to become incarcerated or dead at an early age.

On the financial side of the social equation, teaching the value of entrepreneurship is critical to solving the problems mentioned above. Men and women who understand entrepreneurship and the fundamentals of business realize quickly that you do not need a job to provide for your family. They are no different from farmers who know how to grow their own food during difficult times, or carpenters who can build their own homes when they can't afford to buy one. Rather than being consumers and laborers, they gain the ability to become financiers and decision-makers.

There should be a nation-wide consortium of entrepreneurship programs for black children. Young men and women of color should be expected to attend one of these programs for some period of time and learn the value of creating a business. In the course of such a program, they should be taught how to manage money, how to create a business plan, how to obtain financing

160

and how to partner with others who also have good ideas. We should force our children at an early age to learn how to earn their own money with the opportunities around them: if you see that everyone is thirsty, you start a lemonade stand. If you see that there is snow on the ground, you go door-to-door shoveling snow. Teaching our youth where money comes from is as critical as teaching them where babies come from.

Teaching the value of education as a tool for economic empowerment is critical as well. I call upon the hip hop community to use the power of rap music to emphasize the value and impact of education. This work is already being done, but you can never do enough of it. When I speak to youth about the value of education, I turn to the impact that education has on the students' economic future. I don't judge the kids on why they might want to go to school; I simply encourage them to use school as a tool to help them get what they want and need.

Remember: our kids already know how to work hard. The myth about our youth being lazy, unfocused or uncommitted to anything productive could not be further from the truth. One only needs to go to McDonald's and watch the kids rushing around behind the counter for 10 hours a day to realize that these kids know how to work hard to get what they want. Money motivates them because many of them don't have much of it. The key is to get them to apply this same energy to things that are going to magnify their long-term benefit.

To expand on this idea further, I want to address the myth that those who go to college are simply harder working than those who do not. There is an idea that if you are simply willing to put in the work, you will be successful. On the other hand, some believe that if you fail, it is because you do not have the work ethic necessary to succeed.

I have taught on many college campuses, some of them with tuition rates as high as $30,000 per year. I have seen the best of the best and the worst of the worst. I have spoken at prep schools, prestigious universities, penitentiaries and the worst schools in "the hood." What I've realized is that there is a universal spirit which exists in all ambitious people, making them willing to do whatever is necessary to become successful. There is also a universal spirit in those unwilling to make sacrifices for the future. These spirits (both positive and negative) know few racial, gender or socioeconomic boundaries. The only thing that varies from one economic class to another is the willingness of those around the individual to work overtime to dampen or heighten their spirit to achieve.

I've seen students at private universities who are as pathetic as they come. The George Bush types of the world are no better, no more ethical, and no more ambitious than individuals who decide to live a life that is destitute, crime ridden or parasitic on their communities and those around them. It takes more intelligence to survive in a penitentiary than it does to make it on a college campus, and the consequences of failure are 100 times greater in "the hood" than in middle class America. The black community suffers because many of our greatest geniuses are locked away in these penitentiaries. Some are locked away because they made the wrong choices in spite of having several options. Many of them are there for making the right choices in a world that gives them few options.

The bottom line is that whether you are speaking about a welfare recipient in a housing project or a welfare recipient at an Ivy League university waiting for daddy to send a check every month, the same ideologies apply and the same methods of analysis should be used. The notion that kids in the hood don't have the right values or are just stupid in the choices denies their humanity by presuming that all of us would not consider making some of those same choices if we were in that situation. The first step toward connecting with our children and teaching them the values necessary to embrace their opportunity set is to accept and respect their humanity. The truth is that they, like you and me, are rational economic beings who respond to the world around them.

So, I would argue that the greatest challenge to the black community is not to get inner city youth to change their value systems. It's not to teach the lazy and weak to become workaholics, because these kids are not lazy and weak. It is to simply get them to turn their powerful work ethic in a direction that is sure to provide long-term benefits. It is to get them to realize that with an education, you can do the same amount of work and receive 2 – 4 times more pay than you would receive as an unskilled laborer. It is to get them to realize that no matter what you do, you are going to have to work hard for the next 50 years. The question is whether you want to be paid well for your labor or paid poorly. When education is put into that context, it goes from being an unnecessary evil to a tool for the attainment of the things they deem most valuable. Once the child has been sold on the value of education, you don't have to motivate them any longer.

After our youth are convinced that education is important for them, one must go through the process of breaking down all the mis-education they've received. You must power through the deformed psychological constructs that have been created by a system that does not see value in these children. You have to counter nearly every conversation they've had with teachers, counselors, relatives or friends who tell them that certain educational and personal achievements are not possible. You have to open the door for a psychological rebirth.

The brainwashing of a horrible school system can be difficult to erase, but it is critical that we try. Personally, I tell kids that no matter where you come from, what your grades are or what your skill level is, college can be for you. I tell them that if you are 18 years old and can't read, you can take remedial classes at the local community college and start preparing yourself for college attendance at the age of 21. I explain that the amount of time spent daily to get through school is far less than the 8 – 10 hours per day they would spend working in a factory, a field or a fast food restaurant. I tell our kids that even if they've been labeled by the school system to have a behavioral or learning disorder, there are laws to protect the disabled, thus allowing them to attend college as well. All of the universities at which I've taught have laws that protect students with ADHD and other disabilities by giving them extra time on exams. These students graduate with the same degree as everyone else, and their future employers usually have no idea they were considered disabled during college.

The point is that our kids can do it if we believe in them. I grow tired of going to inner city schools to hear counselors, both black and white, tell me that "college ain't for everybody." All the while, I go to the suburbs to see intellectually and motivationally challenged individuals like George W. Bush being sent to Ivy League institutions. It is time to end the hypocrisy. It is time to kill the lie. It is time that we take our children to the financially empowered futures they deserve. It is up to us, because if we don't do it, no one will.

Chapter 14

The Financial Slavery and Anger of the Black Middle Class

There exists a long list of perceptions on the source and meaning of "the angry black man" or "the angry black woman." Both of these stereotypes draw the fear and ire of a country that is trained to be afraid of black people who stand strong in the face of challenges and adversity. In fact, our society is designed to crush their spirits. Rather than assuming that some of us have a reason to be angry, there are those who choose to stigmatize the anger of black people, while legitimizing their own disappointment.

When I used to watch Lou Dobbs on CNN, I noticed that there is a different reaction toward angry white males than there is when a black man expresses the same degree of indignation. If Lou Dobbs were black, I believe he would have been banned from television a long time ago. But as a middle-aged white male, his anger is thought to be both justified and legitimate. I don't get upset about this hypocrisy, for black people have endured double standards for centuries. Rather, I see it as a simple fact of life. After being on nearly every major network in America, it is my firm belief that there is certainly a strong media bias against people of color. Most of the major news networks do not have a single host that is African-American. Some of them have brought on black co-hosts or a black guest or two, but African-Americans are, for the most part, shut out of these institutions.

This shut out leads to a tremendous bias in the stories that are covered and which stories are considered important. It impacts the angles and perspectives of featured news stories as well. I remember being called by a major network to discuss black women and breast cancer. I was excited to discuss this topic on the air because I have known for a while that breast cancer is a leading cause of death among black women. I thought about the women who matter most in my life: my grandmother, my mother, my sister and my daughter. I also thought about all the daughters, mothers, sisters and grandmothers who exist throughout the nation, and I was honored to have the opportunity to be part of such an important discussion.

At the last minute, one of the producers called me on my cell phone. She informed me that the topic of the show had been changed at the last minute. Rather than discussing black women and breast cancer, they were going to discuss Paris Hilton's latest stint in rehab. I thought "Wow, that's amazing. We went from discussing a leading cause of death among black women to analyzing Paris Hilton's pathetic life." This was yet another reminder that our nation suffers when the minds of the population are controlled by media outlets that have neglected their social responsibility.

There are those who call black people racist for demanding our own media outlets. I am not sure if there is any fair alternative when most of the existing media outlets do not reflect our views, our issues or even put black faces on the air. An important dimension of wealth building is the ability to control media using such outlets to define issues that are relevant to our culture and society. Such media would be inherently designed to give voices to those we choose as leaders, since white-owned media tends to choose African-American leadership on our behalf.

While most black people in general are shut out of white media, angry black people certainly need not apply for the job. If you search every outlet in America, you will never find a black Lou Dobbs fighting hard for issues that affect people of color. Instead you are likely to find those like "The black Avenger," Ken Hamblin, who fight hard for whites who dislike black people. Individuals such as Hamlin have a free ticket to the top of the media hierarchy. The same is true for guys like Larry Elder, who make themselves rich and famous for their attacks on African-Americans. Even Senator Barack Obama learned that attacking black people was a great way to get additional votes during the 2008 Presidential election.

Part of me doesn't blame these men for attacking poor black people. I truly think that some of them actually believe what they are saying. If you've never been around good black people who are poor, then your sheltered life will likely lead you to have the same perception of African-Americans that everyone else gets from watching us in mainstream media. A well-behaved, well-educated black child in the suburbs whose only exposure to black Americans in "the hood" consists of guns, drugs, and a lack of education (all conveniently provided by white-owned media outlets) is certainly not going to want to be a part of that. He is going to consider himself the exception to the rule and special because he doesn't act like "the rest of those people."

The black child from the suburbs will be embraced by his white friends who see him as being different from the black people they fear. Some in the black community make it worse for this individual when they themselves

167

have embraced the negative imagery of black folks, one that consists of a lack of education and little commitment to common sense: Perhaps they make fun of his proper grammar or educational aspirations and apply other self-destructive stereotypes perpetuated by both blacks and whites together. So, they too may make the young black male in the suburbs feel uncomfortable with black people. Like anyone else, this young man is going to spend his time where he is wanted, loved and respected. He may even secretly consider himself to be a white man with black skin. Having few black male role models in mainstream media certainly doesn't help the case. His best bet might be Barack Obama.

That is where the Ken Hamblins come from. I don't believe they hate all black people. They just hate the ones they see on TV or those who come from places they do not understand. Rather than having the necessary exposure to realize that those in "the hood" are as diverse as any other group of people, they have found whiteness to be a haven of comfort, clarity, purity and understanding which lies in stark contrast to the nastiness, poverty, inferiority and filth they perceive to represent the black community.

What is also ironic, however, is that the Ken Hamblins and Ward Connerlys of the world are facing a double-edged sword. While they and much of the black community have grown further apart, they are never fully accepted by many members of the white community, some of whom have come to subconsciously embrace black inferiority. Many black conservatives jump through hoops to impress white females, many of whom would never consider dating a black man. They work especially hard to rid themselves of any residuals of non-mainstream black culture from their youth or households in order to make white men feel comfortable around them.

A great example is that of Michael Steele, the short-lived African-American head of the GOP. Steele seems to believe in his party and while I find his politics to be problematic, I don't question his loyalty to the Republicans. Having a black chairman was a predictable, but relatively effective Republican response to the election of Barack Obama. They seemed to believe that by giving power to a man with a black face, they would become the hip and courageous party that America wanted them to be.

The problem was that the Republicans were trying to be something they were not. They seemed to believe that the black head of the GOP would be able to outweigh the racist dispositions of Sean Hannity, Rush Limbaugh and the rest of the Republican Axis of Ignorance. Soon after Steele's appointment as chairman, he found himself in a verbal war with Rush Limbaugh. The party didn't stand behind Steele and he eventually resigned. Allowing a racist like Limbaugh to hijack the Republican Party and force the resignation of Michael Steele only confirmed what the rest of us already knew: Although Steele wanted to believe the Republicans truly supported him, he was never going to have any real power in a party that doesn't respect African-Americans.

The cultural dilution many African-Americans endure in order to fit into white America leads to challenges that actually make me feel sorry for some, not all, black conservatives and social contortionists. After jumping through every hoop and embracing every challenge, many of them are still passed up for promotion by a white male. This rejection, after you've done everything you need to do in order to prove your loyalty, leads to anger. This anger can even breed insanity, as it is difficult to accept punishment when you have done all the right things. Not knowing who you are, and not knowing where to turn when you are challenged by racism can have an impact on your mental stability. So, the anger of the black middle class isn't just shared by those who have a strong racial identity. It is also felt by those with little identity at all.

The black middle class is an interesting topic of discussion. I have spent a great deal of time around the black middle class, since my parents rose to the middle class during my teenage years. I spent plenty of time around those willing to do whatever it took to experience the American dream. They went to college, bought homes, and became beacons of light for their families, some of whom were still stuck in poverty. Most armchair activism, if any, took place around the dinner table, with the "you know how white folks can be" conversations that occur in the homes of many African-Americans. The 400-year habit of being constantly fearful of white American social terrorism shows itself well in these conversations, because these discussions would never happen outside the walls of the home.

I remember family barbecues in which we would drive to Grandma's house in "the hood," to see a smorgasbord of relatives from all different backgrounds: the cousin who sells crack, the uncle who drinks too much, the sister who became a big shot attorney downtown, and the older brother who just finished his PhD. Those who "made it" earn bragging rights from relatives who are proud of their achievements, and get the attention of those relatives who want to borrow money.

While the American dream seems to have been fulfilled by many members of the black middle class, there is a tremendous amount of anger that comes with the social migration necessary to move into the domain of white men. We teach at universities that don't hire black faculty.

We work for corporations in which we are the only black manager within a 100-mile radius. We are constantly scolded if we are found behaving "too black" in a given setting. There is even a "black tax" for those found associating with too many African-American colleagues. The truth of the matter is that the sacrifice of the black middle class is that many of us are forced to exist in an environment that was built and developed to promote the success of white men. We are, for the most part, invited guests in someone else's home.

I am led to recall the semester in which I took my first faculty position at Syracuse University. The prior year, the entire business school had zero African-American faculty members. All of our students had been, for years, expected to go through 4, 6 or 8 years of college and graduate school without having one single black professor. Personally, I've never had a black professor in any class I've taken, which is astonishing, especially because I spent eight years in graduate school after doing four years of college (yes, I might have a bit too much education, but it has served me well). For some reason, many people have accepted this deformed reality to be the norm and expectation for most American universities. Through an initiative on central campus here at Syracuse, three black business school faculty members were simultaneously hired.

To some extent, we felt like adopted stepchildren. It was made clear from the financial arrangement that our departments were not willing to purchase our services at full price. Rather, a subsidy from central campus was necessary to pay half our salaries. So, like our ancestors, who were considered to be 3/5 of a person, we were considered to be ½ a faculty member.

171

The segregation was strong and immediate. When academic departments add cultural diversity, it is not always to get a diversity of ideas. Many times, there is an expected degree of conformity that comes with the position, one which says that if you do what others around you do and you do it well, you will then be rewarded. I can at least give our country credit for the fact that a black man who behaves as white men do can be just as successful as many white males. Senator Barack Obama, for example, is allowed access to opportunities and offices that are inaccessible to the majority of white males, as long as he's willing to "let all that black stuff go."

In our role as academic stepchildren, we were thrust into an environment in which we had no power. Yes, we had jobs, but there were no senior faculty around to advocate for us. No one considered the possibility that black scholars might have a unique set of issues to fight for and a unique set of challenges. We were expected to publish in so-called "elite journals"; none of them run by black people. These journals are essentially controlled by white men, all of whom are in the "good old boy network", which takes care of its own. None of us had been invited into these networks, so even outstanding scholarly work was going to be rejected.

Soon after our hiring, one of the members of the faculty, a strong black male scholar who was very popular with students, was released for not fulfilling the research expectations of the university. He had tried to get his work published in the "elite journals," but had it consistently rejected. Publishing in black journals would not be considered acceptable, because black journals are not thought to be relevant to true scholarship. The problem is that black men and women were not invited into academia during the period in which journal quality was being determined.

Like the black children in inner city schools, black scholars around the country (including Cornel West and Michael Eric Dyson) are being told that we are not good enough. Personally, I wasn't going to have it. I've worked too hard and sacrificed too much to allow anyone to tell me that I am not as good as the average white male in my department. I responded (politely) by telling the university that I refuse to accept their evaluation of my credentials. I stated, again calmly and respectfully, that an institution (my business school) that has not recommended a black man or woman for tenure in 120 years must prove that it is qualified to evaluate such individuals without bias. The reality was that the historical evidence was overwhelmingly in my favor.

My experience is not much different from that of African-Americans in medicine, law and other professions. Many of the so-called prestigious law firms have never hired a black person and don't plan to hire one in the future. The argument is that they can't find any qualified black attorneys for the position, when the reality is that no one has taken a look at the criteria, or how and when the criteria were created. If I and other black men were allowed, 100 years ago, to decide what work is "qualified" and what work is not, white men would be at a huge disadvantage. Many of the criteria for success in academia includes such arbitrary concepts as "collegiality" (a term used in academia quite often to eliminate people of color from consideration for certain jobs), which mostly reflects your ability to be well-liked in a given environment. Such measures are patently unfair and subject to the cancer of racial exclusion that continues to plague our nation.

One point of confusion for the angry black middle class is that we did not do anything wrong. We are not "Bill Cosby

Rejects" who made all the wrong choices. We did the right thing: we got educated, raised our children and dodged the landmines of the criminal justice system. But the reality is that many of us feel the same anger that young black men feel in the school and prison systems. We pay all the dues and get none of the rewards. We quietly give our services to institutions that would never even consider having an African-American chancellor or CEO. What's worse is that our commitment to financial slavery and desire to chase carrots of the establishment only further serves to muffle our anger and heighten our frustration.

Conversations are had around the dinner table with educated African-Americans that cannot and will not be held in public. I sit every other day with educated blacks who speak all day about how things are unfair and how they did the right things to get the wrong results. Many of them look around and wonder why their campus or corporation continuously makes excuses for their perpetual failure to hire people of color. They know it's wrong because one cannot look at the glaring statistics, as well as the many black scholars seeking positions and find any cause other than racial exclusion. But in spite of all of this indignation, black scholars must remain silent. There is a clear understanding that even if your anger is legitimate, you do not want to be labeled as "the angry black man" or "angry black woman." To portray such anger is the death of your career.

I am here to let the cat out of the bag. Educated black folks are *mad*. Many educated doctors, lawyers, dentists and history teachers are angry that they live and work in a world that does not love or respect them for who they are. Senator Barack Obama, I dare say, is an angry black man. His campaign trail speech on Rev. Jeremiah Wright (before he disavowed his association with Wright) allowed for one of the smallest, yet boldest exhibitions of black anger in a public forum by a high ranking black public official. After being blasted for his association with a pastor who portrayed righteous frustration toward a country that has denied both he and his people fundamental civil rights, Obama was asked to disown the pastor politically and denounce their friendship and association. In a move that would cost him many votes and perhaps the election, Obama refused. He was then hit with a backlash from right-wing racists who felt that he was not American enough to be President of the United States. Eventually, he was pressed harder by the right-wing and denounced Wright completely. The transformation of Barack Obama, in response to this pressure, is similar to the transformation of many African-American professionals around the country.

Barack Obama, who had been processed as a mild mannered "good black man" that the country could love, was backed into a corner nearly every week by Senator Hillary Clinton and the right-wing during the 2008 Presidential election. Every time a small amount of that black middle class anger showed its ugly head, Obama was taken to task. He was asked to denounce the Minister Louis Farrakhan, the epitome of angry black men, when it was found that Obama's pastor's daughter had been connected to an award given to Farrakhan. That is how ridiculous the election got for all of us, and it shows how ridiculous the tap dance can become for African-Americans seeking positions of power.

One interesting aspect of middle class black anger, which I have experienced firsthand, is that we are all afraid of the stigma. None of us are willing or interested in being labeled as "the angry black man" or "angry black woman," even when we have a reason to be mad. Part of the reason we run from the label is because perceptions matter. We want our oppressors to love us. We want to get that corporate promotion. We want to be considered a "good guy" or a "good woman" for the firm. Even in the slums of America, the happy prostitute is always the well-paid prostitute: the evil, bitter prostitute who complains about his or her pimp and doesn't smile during sex is the one who is not going to be well-paid.

The problem with the backward logic of wishing to obtain favor with our historical oppressor is that in the fight for racial equality, it is difficult to fight against oppression and always maintain favor with those who are oppressing you. That is similar to confronting a bully and then worrying that he may get mad at you for punching him. It doesn't mean that you go looking for trouble, but in an honest fight against tyranny, you are drawing a clear line in the sand that says "This behavior is no longer going to be acceptable." The same is true for any abused woman in a bad marriage. She has to stand up to her husband and simply accept the fact that there are going to be points where her decision to stand up is not going to sit well with him. If she is seeking his approval while consistently demanding fairness, she will find herself accepting unacceptable compromises and ultimately chasing her own tail.

That is the experience of the black middle class American in this country, as we have become confused by American double talk on racial inequality. On one hand, there are statements that tell us that America is a land of equal opportunity and that African-Americans are invited and respected guests at the table. This message is contradicted by the one in which egregious statistical imbalances pertaining to wealth, education and job opportunities are allowed to persist with white America simply casting the blame onto black Americans.

For example, most of us have heard statements such as "XYZ Corporation is really looking for minorities. If you have a good grade point average, everybody's gonna want to hire you." The truth of the matter, however, is that many corporations would not have a dearth of black representation if they truly cared about correcting this imbalance. Many academic departments in American universities that have never hired or tenured a black professor will be glad to say that they are aggressively hunting for qualified minority candidates, but every candidate who applies just doesn't seem quite right. In other words, the actions are not consistent with the words coming out of the mouths of academic and corporate leadership. What they are really saying, at best, is "We would love to have a black person here if he/she is the *right kind* of black person. We must approve of their assimilation efforts before we allow them into our shop.

Most of us spend our entire career chasing carrots. Most of these are economic carrots. In a capitalist society, money rules nearly all things. Our nature and desire to "bling out of control" leads us to think the unthinkable and do things that don't make us feel good about who we are. There are attorneys every year who allow black men to rot in prison because of attorney-client privilege. There are African-Americans who sit and watch their black colleagues get mistreated and say nothing because they themselves are afraid of the whip. They are afraid of losing the carrots, and the carrots are made of gold.

Carrots hanging over our heads make us fearful of sharing righteous outrage over clear injustice. When I was a graduate student, I began to notice, in detail, the inequality which existed around me. I saw how many black men were being sent to prison without just cause or fair representation. I noticed large numbers of black youth being born into poverty. I saw universities and corporations unwilling to hire African-Americans. All the while, universities are unwilling to hire black professors, and white coaches are the first in line to recruit the next big black athlete to win a championship.

I responded to the inequality I saw during graduate school by doing what I felt best: I wrote about it and created dialogue. I asked questions that challenged assumptions that others had made about how black people were simply not supposed to have certain opportunities that were readily available to whites. I got in trouble for saying what I said. People warned me, on a regular basis that I would never get a PhD after running my mouth as a black man, even if what I said happened to be true. Many of the people giving me these warnings were well-intended African-Americans who, themselves, had been "beaten into submission." But I turned to something that I know well: Jesus. I do not buy into man-made, institutionalized religion, but I believe strongly in the existence of a higher power. I consider Jesus to be a man who stood for truth in the face of adversity. He was so connected to God that he would not have been allowed to preach at many churches. He was one who did what was right at any expense, and always stood up for the poor and weak in the face of tyranny. Malcolm X, Muhammad Ali, and Martin Luther King possessed many of these same characteristics, although they did not possess the same purity of purpose and focus in the face of challenges and temptation. However, it's hard to match up to Jesus, although I think that every good man or woman should at least consider trying.

I also know that man does not understand nearly as much as we think we do. We have little or no true knowledge about what is possible and what is not. We warn each other to be afraid and to give up on our dreams, even if we have very little experience with that which we currently fear. Most importantly, we significantly underestimate the potential of ourselves and other human beings to overcome adversity.

Early in my career, I noticed the impact of the carrots. I noticed that most of my elders, in their endless quest for middle class respectability, had been hypnotized by the carrots. I noticed that the carrots forced them to jump the line from "sell ups" to "sell outs." Our campus, the University of Kentucky, was embroiled in a racial controversy during which a young black woman had a knife put to her throat for speaking out against racism. Some students followed the young lady to class, cornered her behind the door and threatened to kill her for speaking out in the student newspaper in response to one of my articles. According to the young woman, she was asked by officials to keep the incident quiet and not in the public eye. The school had just won a trip to the NCAA Final Four and was about to take its army of gigantic black men to face off against the University of Massachusetts. A lot was riding on the game, including a multi-million dollar payday for the university.

The irony was peculiar. On one hand, the university was about to enter the national spotlight and receive a large sum of money via its use of underpaid African-American labor. On the other hand, they were telling a young black woman to keep quiet about the fact that someone had come close to cutting her throat for speaking out against racism in the campus newspaper.

The black students were not having any of this. We engaged in a massive protest and fought the university tooth and nail, until advances were made on the campus in terms of funding for the black Student Union and other long-term initiatives. What was most striking about the situation was that nearly every single black faculty member on campus remained quiet, including the head of Minority Affairs. This was not only disgraceful, but a strong reminder of the cowardice that has served as a tool of survival for African-Americans over several hundred years of intimidation. It was also my first vision into how chasing middle class carrots can steal the very soul God gave you and make you socially impotent.

When I was a master's student, people said I should delay speaking out until I'd earned admission into a PhD program. When I was a PhD student, people told me that I was speaking out too early because I needed to first earn my doctorate. When I got my doctorate, people said that I should delay speaking out until I earned tenure. I noticed early that the carrot chase would never end unless I chose to stop it. I also knew that Dr. Martin Luther King died at the age of 39, so the truth was that I wasn't even sure if I had much time left.

Very early in my career, I chose to let go of the carrots. Like a soldier preparing for battle, I knew that the swift and nimble warrior must release all baggage that might slow him down. In the case of the African American, there is a great deal of cultural and social baggage resulting from the need for white validation, the need for wealth, and the desire for status within predominantly white institutions. All of these forms of social drudgery weigh down the African-American political warrior in his or her fight for justice.

Before I got my PhD, I gave one to myself. After making sure that I had taken the appropriate number of classes and had the expertise necessary to justify a doctorate, I proceeded to make a certificate on my home computer. I then put the certificate on my wall and said "I am now Dr.

Boyce Watkins, because I know I earned it. I am not going to wait for someone else to validate me."

Years later, when I was the only African-American in the United States, to my knowledge, to get a PhD in Finance during my year of graduation, I wasn't all that excited. I simply figured that my institution's decision to grant me a PhD was a simple acknowledgment of something I'd known all along: I am a scholar. I didn't need anyone to tell me that I was a scholar, for I see one every day when I look in the mirror.

After getting my doctorate, I let go of any concern whatsoever about making tenure. Not that I would pass it up if it were offered, but I almost never entered into those prolonged and dull academic conversations about all the stupid political tricks one must play in order to get tenure. I had too much work to do and my goal was to be a scholar, not another academic political monkey. I wasn't interested in sitting around biding my time, being quiet about critical issues, all for the goal of obtaining artificially constructed and minimally impactful academic "prestige." Tenure, to me, has never been much more than welfare for highly educated people. The notion that I would give up every ounce of my intellectual and spiritual freedom in exchange for a lifetime job was nonsensical. I'd grown up in an environment where having any job was a wonderful thing. As long as I had a roof over my head, food to eat and a computer to write my books, I was going to be okay.

This is not to insult those who've worked hard to earn tenure, for I am proud of them. But I'd be lying if I didn't say that I've always felt that the pursuit of tenure has been highly overrated, particularly among black scholars. Most of us don't even know why we want tenure so badly. We simply chase it and make every compromise imaginable to obtain it, all because someone told us that this is what we should want. This is NOT the prize. The prize, in my opinion, is to be a liberated and productive intellectual.

Unfortunately, given that the most meaningful work of the black intellectual is not correlated with the mandates of predominantly white universities, the pursuit of tenure often times becomes a deadly academic distraction for those scholars whose work is needed in the black community. The earning of tenure is not, in many cases, a reliable proxy for high impact scholarly work, especially for black scholars. We spend our lives chasing tenure, higher salaries and endowed chairs, only to find that the number of black lives we've impacted is miniscule. But we die feeling successful because white America told us that we are significant. I've always felt that cutting to the chase and providing my own validation beforehand would allow me to focus on work that actually means something.

Letting go of the carrots made me feel every bit as liberated as a woman does when she cuts off her hair. Many women cut their hair because they are tired of poisoning their heads with disgusting chemicals and enduring the pain and expense of one stylist visit after another, all for the approval of men. I felt the same way. I was going to work hard, publish and be a great scholar. But I wasn't working for political approval of anyone other than the people I am here to serve: African-Americans who believe in progressive thought and action. I did not want to be a dean. I did not want to be department chair, and I did not want to be a university president. I knew that the pursuit of such carrots breeds nothing but one political game after another, causing one to deviate from the true purpose of pure scholarship and intellectual leadership.

Letting go of carrots can be costly. As I write this book, I know that my work has angered a university with a business school that has not recommended tenure for a black Finance Professor in its entire 130-year history. I continuously endure evil looks from colleagues who saw me speak on CNN the night before and wish that I would just go away. But the truth is that I am here and I have a purpose. Also, the reality is that there is a price to be paid when one is pure to their discipline. Jesus could not have been a pastor at most churches because he was truly committed to serving God. Einstein was not allowed to teach at many universities because his theories were too radical.

While I do not consider myself to be as great as Jesus, Einstein or anyone else, the truth is that one cannot expect to be different, radical and ground-breaking without enduring a tremendous backlash. There is little institutional incentive to promote and support an individual who fights for causes that are not in your best interest. When I speak out about the NCAA's financial raping of the black community, this causes my university to lose money. It causes black athletes to start asking questions they would not otherwise ask. It causes the university to receive calls from wealthy alumni asking that I be fired. I understand fully why they have no incentive to support the work that I do.

What keeps me going, in spite of the obstacles, is that I realize that this is bigger than one person. The fight for racial equality should not be a selfish fight, laced with our natural quest for glory and recognition. It is like a football game, one that requires tremendous sacrifice, focus, endurance and teamwork. The lineman in a football game plays a critical role in creating the hole for the running back. Without the sweat, blood and grit of the lineman who is willing to put his entire body on the line, the running back has nowhere to go with the ball. However, while the linemen make the greatest sacrifice, they are not the ones who get the opportunity to dance in the end zone. Instead, they end up with no recognition, with their faces smashed into the ground.

What's worse is that the running back may never thank the lineman for his sacrifice. He may feel that his success belongs to him, and that there is no sacrifice greater than his own. Some linemen may be offended, rightfully so, by the attitude of the running back. At the same time, if the lineman truly understands his value and has an honest commitment to the advancement of the team, he will still do his best to block for the running back to try to win the game.

I have always enjoyed playing the role of intellectual lineman. I love it when white America gets angry at me for speaking the truth, because I know it creates opportunities for others. Their desire to prove me wrong or to ostracize me is then balanced with their decision to hire and promote other African-Americans who say the right things. While many of these individuals take advantage of the political benefits of staying away from me, I am still happy for their success. I noticed, for example, that during the year of my tenure case here at Syracuse University, in which many prominent scholars from around the country were writing to support my case, the university began hiring a lot of African-Americans for prominent positions on our campus. There was a new black person on the website every week. They began touting and promoting their initiatives with the inner city. I do not feel this is a coincidence. It is a statement to say "You see, we're not as racist as that guy says we are. Look at the black people we are hiring!"

All of these actions led me to smile. Even though I had reason to believe that the administration was telling people to stay away from me, I was incredibly happy for the success of other African-Americans. I knew that many of the administrative positions were not true positions of power, but I took pride in seeing progress. I had achieved my goal: to transform my university into something that it would never have been had I not arrived. I can now move forward with my career, perhaps to another location, perhaps to another field altogether, and play golf with my father until he gets old.

I admit that I am a very confident man. I believe that confidence in the black male is critical in order to challenge the shackles of white supremacy. I make no apologies for being proud of who I am. However, this confidence should not be confused with arrogance or self-righteousness. I am one who shines his light brightly in the world, but only in hopes that I can get others to shine their light as well. I might be considered by many of my colleagues to be an "uppity negro". I might get the neck-swinging response from other black people thinking, "Who in the hayell does he think HE is?" But I can say with all honesty and humility that I do not believe I am better than anyone else. At the same time, I am the first to admit that there is NO ONE who is better than me.

Chapter 15

Subprime Lending and Retirement Issues

The subprime lending and financial crises of 2008 - 2009 are great examples of capitalism gone wild in America. These crises were, of course, magnified in the black community. Many middle class African-Americans, who had desperately worked to pursue the American dream, found themselves homeless. This process began with individuals being duped into signing on for mortgages on homes they could not afford. The homes appeared to be priced properly, as the payments were made to look as though anyone could afford them. Rather than finding more appropriate investment vehicles and settling for modest homes, millions of us worked overtime to prove to our mamas that we had "made it."

As all parties do, the "Mortgage Freaknik" came to an end. Millions of Americans lost their homes, partly as victims of alleged predatory lending practices of companies that were given a financial boost by the government shortly thereafter. Wells Fargo, one of the primary sponsors of The State of the black Union Conference, was one of them.

The subprime lending crisis was partly created by one of the greatest critics of the Federal Reserve Board, former Federal Reserve Board Chairman Alan Greenspan. During the 1990s, Greenspan put mechanisms into place that amounted to a welfare office for large banks. If the banks took excessive risk and failed, they knew that Greenspan would bail them out. Years later, this created a "speculation bubble" in the housing market, which led to home prices spiraling out of control. As all bubbles do, this one burst in 2008, leading to declining real estate valuations, causing one foreclosure after another. African-Americans were right in the middle of this crisis; well, actually we were on the bottom of it. Many of us were living great lifestyles, but these styles were skating beautifully on very thin ice. We didn't realize that living paycheck to paycheck is even more devastating when your paycheck is large. We also found that not having savings or retirement plans would eventually cause financial chickens to come home to roost.

I argue that many of these poor financial habits derive from the fact that a large number of members of the black middle class did not grow up with a great deal of family wealth. Many of us have never received an inheritance, we are the strongest earners in our families, are saddled with student loans, and were never taught the difference between income and wealth. I do not fault members of the black middle class for these problems, as these realities are the consequence of our nation going several hundred years without allowing black families to pass wealth to their children. At the same time, the cycle has to be reversed at some point, and the verdict is mixed as to whether or not the children of the black middle class are being taught the right values as they move to the next generation.

The values of hard work and perseverance can sometimes disappear as one climbs the economic ladder. The spoils of success can make us financially fat, slow and lazy. The reality is that many children with parents in the black middle class do not embody the same values that their parents used to obtain their relative prosperity. What is most problematic is that our declining commitment to hard work is going to have a double impact on our children, as their parents have not properly planned for retirement.

Many children of the middle class are raised with the mindset of welfare recipients. They are sent to college and invited back home with open arms in the event that things don't work out. The youth are encouraged to depend on their parents well into their late 20s and even their 30s. Many parents don't mind being financial strongholds for their children, because they are earning relatively high incomes. Their 40s and 50s are peak earning years, so the money flowing from the financial faucet provides financial security for everyone.

The problem is when the baby boomers begin to retire. This is typically the point at which intergenerational wealth transfers take place, the children become the parents, and the parents rely on retirement savings to get them by. The problem with this scenario is multifold.

First, the parents of America have not been saving for retirement. The baby boomer generation has failed in the test of wealth management. It too has been swept up in the bliss of American prosperity, living paycheck to paycheck and enjoying "the good life." Even factory workers have been able to enjoy solid wages (which they should receive), nice homes and frivolous spending. I was shocked to see how many employees were willing to take the buyout offered by General Motors in 2007. For $120,000, the firm bought out the contracts and all future financial obligations from tens of thousands of employees after posting a record loss of $38.3 billion dollars.

The problem in the GM buyout was that the annual cost to the firm per employee, including retirement, salary and benefits, was $148,000 per year. So, the employees sold their present and future for $120,000 in cash. The logic behind the decision for many workers was simple: credit cards were overdue; kids were in college; there were vacations to take; and new cars to purchase. The cash was immediately put to use.

It is my firm expectation that the United States is on its way to a retirement crisis unlike any other we've ever seen in our history. While I speak in more detail in later chapters about the retirement crisis, I can say at this point that it is going to have its greatest impact on the black community. Even the black middle class will not be spared from the pain. The bigger your paycheck, the harder you fall in America, where we've always felt that financial security was a birthright.

Second, if there is no retirement savings, there is certainly not going to be any transfer of intergenerational wealth. One would hope and expect that this period of unprecedented black economic prosperity would lead to greater wealth building in the black community. It is the hope and dream of all African-Americans that higher paychecks and a greater perch on the top of the corporate ladder would lead African-Americans to be able to do something that many of their parents were not able to do: leave something for their children.

In some cases, there is plenty of wealth to be shared. Families who have paid off their homes and properly planned for retirement are able to leave something behind, thus improving the economic plight of their families. But for others, poor financial planning and a lack of retirement preparation leads many of these families to run out of resources before they pass on.

The truth in retirement planning is that most people underestimate their financial needs. They don't realize that one needs to have roughly 10 times their annual income in retirement savings in order to be properly prepared. I go into detail on retirement planning on our blogs, but the important thing that many people forget is that retirement is not the beginning of the end. Rather, it can be a second life in which you are expected to spend that second life living off of your savings, pensions and social security. For those who are unable to live even 3 months without a paycheck, one wonders how they are going to survive another 10 – 20 years.

Third, many of our children have not been raised with sound financial values and are not in a position to provide for their elderly parents. In fact, many of them are still dependent on their families for income, draining the retirement resources that have been put in place. I personally know a man in his forties, with a mother in her 70s. He does not have a phone and he only lives in the same location for 2 – 3 weeks at a time. I don't write his number in my phone book because I know that it's going to change within a couple of weeks. His life is a web of instability that won't stop until he's dead.

This young man was never taught what it means to be a man. He never learned the importance of providing for elderly parents as they age. He always saw his mother as the financial rock of the family, because she has always been a good saver. He doesn't see his consistent leaching for what it is: a burden on those he claims to love the most.

While he never learned to be financially responsible, he was never forced to mature. He graduated from high school never having had a job or any other form of true accountability. He went to college for 5 months, fully on his parents' dime, and came home after he chose to party hard instead of going to class. His parents complained, moaned, yelled and screamed, but they ultimately let him move back in the house.

Since the bills were paid, and there was no responsibility, he had little incentive to leave his parents' home. Making matters worse, his mother's empty nest syndrome led her to revert back to the mother-son relationship they'd had decades earlier, in which he was the reckless child with "cute" behavior patterns that were otherwise disturbing. As she did when he was a child, she cooked for him, cleaned for him and never forced him to contribute to the family finances.

The family had a few financial problems, but they were fleeting. Both the mother and the father had good incomes, and they would never share their financial problems with the children. However, there was a dirty little secret: the parents had not planned for their own retirement and were one paycheck away from being broke.

When the young man's father was laid off from a major automobile manufacturer, this led his father into a deep depression, serious drinking and major health problems. He died soon after, leaving no insurance to speak of. The family continued to survive, primarily because the man's wife had a good job and the home was paid for. The son, seeing himself as the helpless member of the family, never thought it was his role to step in to support his mother during her financial struggles. Like the helpless child he was raised to be, he never felt that it was his obligation or within his realm of capability to help his mother in tough economic times.

The young man's mother played right into the myth of invincibility she and her husband had been feeding their child over the years. She coddled her son, never asked him to help pay bills and suffered in financial silence for years. Eventually, when she went to a home for senior citizens, her son was still begging his mother for small loans that she would take out of her retirement account. She died broke, and was unable to leave anything to her children.

The bottom line is this: if you give a child a wheelchair before they learn to walk, they will never bother to learn to use their legs. Lessons of financial strength and responsibility must be taught to the child at an early age, not when the child is too old to learn the lesson. Our children can jump hurdles of education and responsibility, and they will only jump as high as we ask them to jump. I encourage all parents to force their children to learn to jump high, which many of us in the black middle and upper class have neglected to do.

Here are some quick thoughts on how to raise a child to become financially responsible:

1) **Never give children money without asking him/her to earn that money. Life doesn't work that way, so why should it work that way for your child?**

We all understand the rules of adulthood: "If you don't work, you don't eat". "You have to pay the cost to be the boss," "To the victor goes the spoils," "He who has the gold makes the rules." In few places around the world are these rules of capitalism truer than they are in the United States of America. Given that you understand these rules fully and know that your adult child is going to be held to these standards of manhood, womanhood and social responsibility, why in the world would you deny him these lessons?

I have a daughter and several godchildren. All of them have asked me for money at some point in time. If we are going out to dinner or the movies, I don't hassle them much about money being spent. But if they ask for a substantial sum of money, say $30 and it is going to be spent at their discretion, my first reaction is to ask what they are going to do to earn those resources. I tell them that nothing in life is free, and the reality is that you must create your own financial opportunities in life by providing something of value in exchange for the value you are requesting.

Again, it's about forming expectations, because our children jump whatever hurdles we set for them. If I were to yank $30 out of my pocket every time my child asked for it, my child would be taught a powerful subconscious lesson: "If I beg for something, then I will get it for nothing." People carry these lessons through life, and the first teachers of these lessons are parents. I see one college student after another at prestigious universities who are well into their 20s waiting for their parents to send them their weekly check. At the same time, these individuals and their families have the audacity to turn their noses up at single mothers on welfare. Your child should not be trained to be a welfare recipient, no matter what their income level.

2) Let your children see your bills

There is an old hip hop song that has says: "A child is born with no state of mind, blind to the ways of mankind." One can interpret these lyrics in a multitude

193

of ways, one of which is to argue that children of any ethnicity are essentially born without any understanding of the world around them. Their natural instinct is to think that they are the center of the universe, and that they have a birthright to everything they want.

It is up to parents to slap their children out of their natural self-centered reality. One area in which that self-centered reality rears its ugly head is in financial relationships.

Children think that lights, gas and rent are free. They think their parents have an endless supply of money to pay for every trip to McDonald's they would like to take. When a little boy watches his mother open her purse, he believes that her pile of $1 dollar bills make her into a billionaire. They see you as their own personal federal reserve bank, with endless amounts of money that you can print in your basement.

One way to help your child gain an appreciation for money is to push him to understand that resources are limited in the household. You don't have to reveal your income, but you can let your child know that you can only pay the bills in the house because you are careful when managing money. Secondly, you can let your child see some of the bills. Show him how much a light, gas or water bill actually is. Show him the price on your mortgage and allow him to overhear you and your spouse discuss how you are going to cover the bills for the month. Hearing these conversations will give your child an early sense of responsibility and understanding of the value of money and the importance of money management.

3) Let your child get a job as soon as possible.

There is NOTHING wrong with hard work. The earlier one is exposed to hard work, the better off they are. Children in third world countries have this advantage and American children do not. While I would much rather live in the United States than most countries throughout the world, the truth is that our children can sometimes become spoiled by the wealth their parents have bestowed upon them.

I recommend giving your child a job when they are 5 years old. Nothing serious, just something that makes them feel responsible. Give them a paycheck for the job, and make the process as similar to your own life as you possibly can. If they don't do the work effectively, they should be penalized. If they work overtime, perhaps they can earn extra pay. Children enjoy this process because it makes them feel like adults, and they get the thrill of earning their own income. You get the additional thrill of knowing that you are raising a financially responsible child.

4) Let your child contribute to their college expenses, even if you can pay them yourself.

A lot of my mother's friends thought she was truly insane. But I guess she showed that there is some salvation that comes along with insanity. When my brother, sister and I were getting ready for college, my mother insisted that we all contribute to the cost of our own education. She argued, convincingly and perhaps correctly, that "grown ass people" should learn to become financially independent as early as possible, and that there is no reason for her to destroy her retirement planning or mortgage her house in order to pay for something that could be afforded via the use of outside resources.

My mother was right. I got a job, and found that I could have far more money with my job and scholarship than I would ever have if I'd sat around waiting for my parents to send me a check. My sister studied medicine at The Mayo Clinic, and my brother was admitted to the MBA program at Cornell University. All of us were able to become financially independent adults without asking my mother for much of anything.

Had my mother taken the alternative approach of coddling us, we would have been different people. We would have seen her resources as the options of first resort rather than last resort. We would have lost because our mother would have never given us the chance to spread our wings and learn to fly. My mother would have lost because she would have been forced to support grown children for the next decade or longer. She would have also lost on having the chance to have 3 financially secure children who could provide her with additional layers of financial support into retirement.

5) Teach your child to balance a checkbook

Most high school students are not taught how to balance a checkbook. Rather than spending so much time reading old English literature that they will never use again, I argue that some of this time be allocated toward teaching the youth something that they can use. The schools are not going to do this for you, you must do it yourself.

Teaching your child how to balance a checkbook is not only easy, it is critical. A person who balances their checkbook tends to keep a closer eye on their financial situation. Losing money is like wasting time....you are less likely to waste it if your eyes are always on your watch.

Given that many Americans now engage in electronic banking, there is still a form of balancing that must take place there as well. Effectively, you would want your child to learn the value of always knowing how much is in the account before shopping with his/her debit card.

6) Give your child incentives to save

Telling your child to save is not always enough. Sometimes you have to actually show them how to do it. I recommend giving your child the option of using you as a bank. Not as a bank where they can get free money, but rather, a bank where they can make deposits and earn interest. If you really want to be creative, you can even give them small loans and collect interest. Thinking through the decision to borrow and invest can be their first introduction to money management. I also recommend paying an interest rate that is higher than most banks. Five percent per year is not likely to get a reaction out of your child. However, 5% per week might do the trick. Don't forget to make it fun.

You can even provide loans for investment projects your child can take on, such as starting a lemonade or newspaper stand. I would also give your child a chance to learn the flaws of borrowing for frivolous investments like more candy, shoes, etc.

7) Teach your child how to create a job

An ability to embrace and understand the value of entrepreneurship is critical to the next step in the quest for equal rights in America. Capitalism does not naturally provide wealth and financial endowments to workers or other sources of labor. Typically, owners are the ones most likely to build wealth from their investment in financial capital. The avenue for the poor tends to be human capital (education and other developed skills), which allows laborers to benefit from capitalism. The use of human capital must be a conscious process in which one explicitly reinvests the money earned from his labor. In other words, you save money from your paycheck and build wealth through investment in real property or some other asset – letting your money start working for you.

These lessons should be taught to your children early in life. Our children should know how to spot opportunities to make money and to create channels for obtaining an income from that opportunity. Most new businesses operate in essentially the same way: they find a need and fill it. The business process can be broken into the following categories:

- Planning the production, marketing, distribution and management processes for your business venture

- Obtaining the financing necessary to undertake the venture

- Producing the product you are going to sell

- Marketing and distributing the product you've created

- Managing the organization that produces, markets and distributes the product

- Planning the reinvestment process which will allow your business to continue to grow

You'll find that most business schools are structured around the following concepts: Management, Marketing, Finance and Accounting. Some universities add departments such as Entrepreneurship, Business Law, etc., but they are more tangential to the four fundamental areas of Business. So, anything that a major corporation does, your child can learn to do the very same thing on a simpler level. For example, if your child wants to open a lemonade stand, the process can be broken up in the following way:

- The lemonade must be produced by getting enough lemons, sugar, water and containers to create the product that will be sold to the customer

- The production must be financed, and the financing can come from multiple sources: a loan from the bank (you may actually perform the role of your child's bank), internal funds (money in the child's savings account), external equity holders in the venture (friends or neighbors who want to invest in exchange for a share of the profits).

- Once production is financed and the product has been created, the customer must be made aware of the product's existence. This might require the child to go through the neighborhood with fliers, or to have someone stand on the corner to call potential customers to the new business. It may also require sending out an email or Facebook message to all of the child's friends who might want to drink some lemonade. This gives the child a chance to understand concepts such as brand building and continued customer awareness, which are critical in marketing campaigns.

- Finally, the product has to be distributed to consumers. This might mean opening multiple lemonade stands at key locations, having employees at each stand ready to pass out cups of lemonade or perhaps going door to door to ask customers if they would like to order a cup of fresh squeezed lemonade.

You can go through these lessons with your child. You can also visit DrBoyceMoney.com to learn these lessons in more detail.

8) Consistently communicate variation in economic outcomes as it pertains to educational attainment.

I am sorry to put it this way, but the truth is that many young kids have trouble understanding why school is important; I know I did. If you are lucky, your kids will value education simply because you tell them that it is valuable. I see one straight-A student after another who works their butt off and has no idea why they are doing it. They just know that their parents tell them that education is important, and like a good soldier, they are simply following orders. Sometimes this works, but not for very long. Having a child who follows orders is never as good as actually showing them the value of education and allowing them to feel it. Then, they want to become educated for their own reasons, not yours.

At worst, you may have a child like me, who only saw going to school as a dull, tedious and annoying process. Like any other rational human being, I didn't want to do things that I did not enjoy. I saw no benefit at the end of the rainbow from attaining education, so I didn't feel the need to become highly educated. I worked hard at football, basketball and track practice because I saw the immediate benefits of working hard in sports: you get the glory and the girls. It was only after I got to college and started to see the rewards that come with education that I started to believe that working hard in school was important.

Had I gotten clear lessons earlier in life about the value of education, I would have worked as hard in school as I did on the basketball court. I could have taken advanced classes as a child and even college courses at the age of 14. All of that ability was within me, but there was no mechanism in place to pull my academic strength to the surface. If I'd been motivated properly, no one would have had to force me to do anything. I would not have needed anyone to remind me to study every day, as I would have done it on my own. Going to school would have been something to look forward to, rather than something to dread.

Parents are the people who can provide that connection between education and economics that is so critical for our children. You can highlight career choices for your child. You can discuss the educational qualifications necessary to work in various professions and explain expected future income levels. I am not one to judge whether you want your child to become a doctor or police officer; such decisions are up to you and your family. But clearly identifying the link between education and economics can help your child make a more informed decision when he/she hits adulthood.

9) Send your child to a camp, class or any kind of activity that teaches money management and entrepreneurship.

You can search the internet to find camps and programs during the summer that focus on teaching children money management. If you don't have money to send your child to such a camp, then invest time into researching ways to teach your children about money. There is no reason you should have to pay someone else to do things you can do on your own. The key is that they learn financial lessons at an early age, and although you may think you don't have the know-how to teach your children, the truth is that you have a lifetime of information that you can share.

10) Teach your child how to value money without overvaluing it

One of the most beautiful things about black culture is that it's not "All about the Benjamins." Things like family, love and community are far more important to many of us. Even the fact that many African-Americans are incredibly quick to enjoy money rather than save it is not always such a bad thing. The other extreme of money management, the one that we consider to be the most appropriate model in a capitalist society, is one that worships money. Some of us choose to become "Money Monsters," where money is the most important thing in the world.

The Money Monster watches shows entirely dedicated to money. The Money Monster's pastor preaches about money in church and accepts donations from any politician willing to offer them. The Money Monster no longer talks to his brother because he borrowed $10,000 from him a few years ago without paying it back. I don't recommend making your child into a Money Monster. Not only does the Money Monster lead an unfulfilling life, he is bored out of his mind. The idea that a child is typically going to want to spend all his time watching Bloomberg and talking about mutual funds and stocks all day is not realistic for most children. Sure there are the black Alex Keatons of the world (a character from the show "Family Ties"), but most children are not in that category.

Money can be taught with a sense of respect and humility. Respecting money implies that you realize that money is a tool for liberation and creative power, if used appropriately. It implies that you realize the good that money can do in your life and the lives of those you love. You understand the machinery behind economic engines that will allow you to create community building institutions that are self-sustaining and profitable enough to grow under their own power. You know how the power of American capitalism operates and it opens your life to endless possibilities.

Teach your children about wealth with humility. The child should understand that having more money than another man does not make your soul anymore meaningful than his. The child should understand that money should never be used as a weapon to destroy relationships with those you love. He should also have the humility and respect for money that reminds him that your greatest wealth is that which lies within your soul, your health, your youth and your personal relationships.

In other words, the lesson must be balanced. So, when teaching your child to balance his checkbook, also teach him to balance his life. As I love to say on a regular basis: Some of the richest people in the world have no money at all, and some of the poorest people in the world have billions.

Chapter 16

Why I despise the NCAA

In the course of writing this book, I have eluded to the long-term battle I've had with the NCAA. I have committed much of my life to this pursuit, and the reality is that I am in this fight for the long-haul. Fortunately, I am not alone. Walter Byers, the former Executive Director of the NCAA, stated in his book "Unsportsmanlike Conduct" that college athletes are being exploited and that they should be compensated for their labor, just like everyone else.

The problem is that you don't have to be an expert to see the exploitation which lies in front of you. You don't even have to have a college education, or financial expertise. Everyone knows what it looks like when someone is getting "pimped." The "pimping" process is simple: those who earn the money are forced to give that money up to someone who did not earn the money. That's collegiate athletics in a nutshell.

You also don't have to be an expert to see that the primary revenue generators in college sports are African-Americans. It is not uncommon to watch an NCAA championship basketball game and see 10 black players on the court. At the same time, both coaches are usually white, and most of the administrators earning revenue from the game are white. The people in the stands are predominantly white, and the faculty and students at the respective universities are white as well.

This reminds one of the Cotton Club environment 100 years ago, when black performers could come in and do a song and dance, while African-Americans were not allowed in the audience. Not much has changed, as the NCAA has unwittingly found itself repeating the darkest parts of America's racially segregated past.

What is most insulting about the structure of collegiate athletics is that half of the black athletes come from poverty. Their mothers are being evicted, their siblings are getting shot, and some of them even take custody of their brothers and sisters in response to challenging circumstances at home. The universities and the NCAA system show no concern for their situation, and only ensure that NCAA assets are protected and provide a good return on investment.

There is an argument and a mythical belief that the NCAA is not obligated to compensate athletes or their families for their huge returns on the court/field because the athletes are amateurs. There is almost nothing that happens in the life of a revenue-generating college athlete that speaks of amateurism: they miss class for games on a regular basis, they are regularly interviewed by media and expected to be as professional as their coaches. They conduct practice on a daily basis in the same business-like manner as professional athletes. The only thing that makes them amateur is that the NCAA says they are.

The Ways and Means Committee of the United States House of Representatives agrees with this assessment. In a letter written to NCAA president Myles Brand, Chairman Bill Thomas had this to say:

> *"The annual return also states that one of the NCAA's purposes is to "retain a clear line of demarcation between intercollegiate athletics and professional*

sports." Corporate sponsorships, multimillion dollar television deals, highly paid coaches with no academic duties, and the dedication of inordinate amounts of time by athletes to training lead many to believe that major college football and men's basketball more closely resemble professional sports than amateur sports."

The NCAA's attitude toward the men and women on the court is one that reeks of racism. When I make the simple argument on radio shows that athletes should get something for their labor that is reflective of their true value to the university, the comments made about student athletes are appalling: "If athletes start to get paid, they're just gonna spend it on gold chains and rims for their cars," or "They should be happy to get a scholarship, which is better than what they were getting before."

The statements being made by those who are against college athlete compensation remind me of the paternalistic nature of Barbara Bush's remarks about Hurricane Katrina victims. Mrs. Bush claimed that the Katrina victims should be happy living in the stadium in which they were housed because it was probably better than the conditions from which they came.

What is also interesting about the comments I hear from the American public as it pertains to the fair compensation of NCAA athletes and their families is that while people are directly and immediately against the idea of providing any compensation to the men and women earning the revenue, they rarely question the level of compensation received by the coaches. They act as though they *deserve it.*

This asymmetric view of collegiate compensation again alludes to the idea that "those big dumb negroes don't deserve anymore than I do," which has been consistent throughout American history. When these young men leave college and come back to their universities to try to become coaches, they are often denied the job. Terry Bowden, a prominent white football coach in the NCAA, made it clear when he explained in a Yahoo Sports article that black coaches are not hired by the NCAA because they are black. In the words of Bowden:

"Many presidents won't hire black coaches because they are worried about how alumni and donors will react."

He also makes this clear and interesting point when it comes to the NCAA's lack of regard for hiring minority coaches:

"There are 117 colleges participating in Division I-A football and there are only three black head coaches. You don't have to be too smart to know how stupid this looks.

Let me lay it out for you:

☐ *Fifty percent black athletes leads to 25 percent black assistant coaches leads to 3 percent black head coaches.*

☐ *Fifty percent white athletes leads to 75 percent white assistant coaches leads to 97 percent white head coaches."*

While the NCAA made tremendous progress in the hiring of Black college football coaches during the 2009 football season, the truth is that there is still a long way to go. Even if Black coaches are being hired, the athletes and their families are still being denied a piece of the NCAA economic pie. Additionally, the power structure of college sports is still out of the hands of African Americans, and the struggle must continue.

The point is very simply put: history is repeating itself, as African-Americans are cast at the bottom of the capitalist totem-pole. We are the laborers and consumers, but not the managers and owners of these establishments. Part of this is due to the history of our country, in which the greatest American institutions were established without our being at the table. However, there is a component of this reality perpetuated by the fact that we have grown comfortable as laborers. We don't get more because we ourselves don't feel that we deserve more. In other words, the "slave mentality" shows itself quite clearly in collegiate athletics, and it is clearly time for a change.

I have seen the stories of many athletes up close, as some of them have lost their scholarships when they wanted to focus on academics. Some have gotten injured or even paralyzed on the field. Many of them have watched their families endure one tragedy after another as they were on national television securing multimillion dollar endorsements for the NCAA.

One player, Francisco Garcia at the University of Louisville, had to deal with his brother being shot and killed as he was taking his team to the Final Four. Francisco's coach, Rick Pitino, received a large financial bonus for the team's performance and the university received a lump sum check in the millions. Francisco wasn't given a check for his performance, he only got a dead brother. Had his family been receiving even a fraction of what Francisco was generating for the university, it is far more likely that his brother would not have been living in the projects getting shot.

Another player, whose name I won't mention here, carried his team to the Final Four as well. His mother wanted to attend the game, but she didn't have the money for a bus ticket. So, her only solution was to go to her church to beg for money to attend the game. What's worse is that if the NCAA had found out about the donations, it would have constituted a violation of NCAA regulations.

I've talked to players about the NCAA situation and some of them are aware of how things work. Many of them are afraid to challenge the system, for good reason. Also, the slave mentality kicks in, as many of us are happy to get whatever we are given. Some athletes play right into the hands of the system, not caring much about getting educated in the first place. That is no crime in my book; I understand why people get scared and I understand that not everyone can see the value of a good education.

What bothers me most about the situation with college athletes is not that they are being ripped off. It's not that they are sometimes choosing to be exploited. It's that they are allowing this corrupt system to steal the most important thing they own: their desire and ability to think and critically analyze.

One enlightened player at a university in the south made things very clear to me with the following statement: "They don't want us to think. That would make us dangerous."

He was absolutely correct. College athletes are soldiers, and no military wants their soldiers to become independent thinkers. However, like a soldier, college athletes are not devoid of the ability to analyze, as they memorize thick play books every season that would put calculus textbooks to shame. However, this thinking is carefully controlled by the university, the same way a pimp carefully controls how his prostitutes think. He wants them to be thoughtful in how they make money and deal with "clients," but these thought processes must be completely along company lines. Any thoughts of independence are quickly squashed under the firm hand of the pimp, who realizes that he must run his organization out of fear in order to keep his prostitutes from rebelling.

Like that same pimp, the NCAA rules college athletes with an iron hand. They are deliberately separated from individuals (like me) who explain the system to them. The NCAA also ensures that these athletes are not being properly educated. When players receive extra money to help their families, they are punished severely, while coaches can receive money on the players' behalf from anyone willing to pay it. When they try to transfer to another university, they lose a year of eligibility, while coaches can switch jobs in the middle of the season. At the time of this writing, a new rule is expected to pass, stating that athletes cannot go to the NBA until they are 21 years old. While this rule is being pushed by the NBA under the paternalistic guise that athletes should be mature before they become professionals, I argue that it is actually a form of collusion between the NCAA and the NBA to further restrict the labor rights of college athletes. For example, the NCAA would have easily earned an extra $50 million dollars or more had Lebron James been forced to show his amazing talents at the college level for free. His mother would have remained poor, but the white administrators and coaches would have become quite wealthy. This is textbook "blacksploitation."

Again, there are those who claim that if athletes don't want to learn, coaches can't make them do it. So, the same individuals and institutions who take full responsibility for making sure that the money is earned and that players are on the floor earning it devoid themselves of any responsibility for making the athletes perform in the classroom. Such an argument stinks of racism, as it implies that these "big dumb negroes" are choosing their own demise. The same arguments are used to describe black boys in the school and prison systems.

The problem with an argument that solely blames athletes for not being educated is that it ignores the impact of university incentives. Athletes are brought to universities with the full expectation that many of them are there only to play sports. Any athlete who rebels from this expectation is quickly punished, because the idea of putting academics in front of athletics sounds good on paper, but is not endorsed in practice. A coach with high graduation rates and a low winning percentage will be fired, but a coach with low graduation rates and a high winning percentage receives a raise and a promotion. This obvious contradiction implies that there are few incentives in college sports for coaches or athletes to make academics a high priority. The reality is that if coaches were financially rewarded for good grade point averages and fired for low grades, they would force their players to study the same way they force them to go to practice.

Educated, courageous and critically-thinking black athletes would be an absolute nightmare for the NCAA. The truth of the matter is that this is yet another textbook reminder that an educated black man scares the heck out of people. The power of athletes, should they work together to confront NCAA exploitation, would be dramatic. It would also serve as a service to the community, because the aggregated wealth extraction from NCAA blacksploitation is over $1 billion dollars per year. This wealth is being taken out of a community that cannot afford to give money away. Additionally, many historically black colleges and universities cannot pay the bills, while some of the most valuable resources in the black community are being yanked away by the busload. Something has to give.

I was once on a CBS Sports special about the NCAA. The goal of the show, according to the producers, was to ask "Should College Athletes be Paid?" I was surprised that CBS called me for this special because CBS is partnered with the NCAA. They signed an 11-year, $6 billion dollar TV rights deal just for the *television production rights* of March Madness. It didn't make sense to me, as a business school professor, that CBS Sports would allow the value of their brand to be jeopardized in that way. Asking such a dangerous, yet obvious question in public could cause serious problems.

While their decision to air the show confused me, I eventually figured out why CBS wanted to air the show. First of all, the show was not to actually ask the question in a genuine fashion. It was to use good old-fashioned communist-era propaganda to explain to the public why college athletes could never be paid. Secondly, I had been on a lot of shows and featured in hundreds of newspapers over the prior weeks explaining clearly why the NCAA should pay its athletes. Appearances on CNN, the LA Times, ESPN radio and hundreds of other media outlets during recent weeks had apparently rattled NCAA officials. I just wanted to address the issue honestly and I wasn't sure how they were going to react.

The third reason I conjecture that CBS Sports was holding this special was very simple: I was an educated black man speaking out about the money, and they had to find a way to counter my public arguments. Most of the critics of the NCAA had been, for the most part, liberal whites who spoke solely on the educational hypocrisy of the NCAA. The NCAA was ready for that, and had a long list of arguments to confront such challenges. But to have a black man speak on the issue brought out the pink elephant in the middle of the room: most of the athletes are black and the black community was being exploited. Racializing the issue opened a whole new can of worms for the NCAA that they could no longer ignore.

Unlike other scholars, I quickly moved past the educational arguments on exploitation. This was not because I don't value education; I feel that education is one of the most valuable things a human being can have. The reality that I saw, as a financial expert, was that the NCAA would be let off the hook if we simply tell them that graduating their athletes would make everything fair. This would feed into the illusion that the NCAA is an academic entity and ignore the fact that a $30,000 per year education is peanuts compared to the millions being earned from college athletes in revenue generating sports. The reality is that many schools earn more money from one national TV appearance than it costs to pay the entire year's tuition for every single player on the basketball team. Education is valuable, but given that many students in poverty go to college in order to earn a living, I find it equally important that they be allowed to take advantage of opportunities to provide for their families.

Rather than talking about education, I talked about THE MONEY. As a Finance Professor, I was able to break down the financial conversation in ways that most academics in the humanities cannot. As an educator, I could talk about the academic fraud that I've witnessed during my 16 years teaching at institutions with large athletics departments. As a black man, I could clearly communicate the ways in which black men, women and children are being exploited and damaged by this system. Having access to the media meant that my ideas would not be hidden away in some dusty academic journal that no one ever reads. They would be made available to millions and legible to the American public. My affiliations with Jesse Jackson, Al Sharpton and others showed that I could reach out and get African-Americans mobilized behind the idea of challenging this exploitation. As a non-traditional scholar, they could easily tell that I would not be afraid of any stigmas that come toward academics that are defined as "critics" or "controversial." I have been known as an angry black man for quite a while now, and I find nothing shameful about being angry, especially if there is an injustice that demands your angry and emotional attention. In some ways, I think the NCAA saw my emergence as the perfect storm.

The CBS sports special was shown right before the Final Four. It featured all the usual suspects and commentators from CBS, including Clark Kellogg, Seth Davis, Len Elmore, "Coach K" (Mike Krzyzewski) from Duke University, Billy Packer, and even NCAA President, Myles Brand. I was surprised that Myles Brand was making a public appearance to discuss this issue. Brand and others are very careful not to put themselves in harm's way when trying to defend the business model of the NCAA. They don't do many interviews and engage in almost no public debates. The only exceptions are cases like this one, in which CBS allowed Brand to be in a safe environment, answering a series of softball questions. No pimp wants to be held accountable in a fair and unbiased forum.

I was the lone critic of the NCAA on the CBS Sports special. I didn't mind taking the role of the lone critic because I am used to it. The show would feature one sound bite from me, and then have 2 – 3 other commentators refuting my words. One other thing I noticed was that whenever I spoke, Clark and Len, both African-Americans, were most likely to be featured right after me. I wondered if they put the black men right behind me in order to de-racialize the issue and "prove" that this exploitation has nothing to do with race. It is a common tactic for racist individuals or organizations to find black people to support their ideas in order to provide the illusion of neutrality or legitimacy. But the truth is that anyone can be bought, including black people. Actually, black people can sometimes be bought for the least, as many of us come from poor families.

The show was an interesting and telling infomercial and communicated clearly to me the urgency being felt within the NCAA. After seeing how the show was edited and the message was conveyed, things started to make more sense. When a good pimp is approached by his prostitutes to explain why he is not sharing the money, he becomes complex and elusive in his explanations. He argues that the cost of doing business is high, that there is not enough revenue for him to share, that the money has been allocated already to another critical venture, and that he is "protecting" the hooker by not sharing the money.

Like a good pimp, the NCAA's responses become equally complicated when athletes call for their share of the money. They cite the fact that many college athletics departments don't have the money to pay the players (even though they always find money to pay millions to coaches), that Title IX, a law ordering gender equity in sport funding precludes their ability to share revenue with players' families (although there is no such regulation in

place for coaching or administrator salaries). They argu_
that they are protecting players with a series of laws, rules
and regulations that control player mobility and access to
opportunity (although this same desire to protect the
athlete goes out the window when the player graduates
and needs help getting a coaching job). Like an academic
Super Fly, the NCAA has a long list of reasons that
college athletes can't possibly get paid. In their
arguments, they make it clear that compensating college
athletes would just be too damn complicated.

One of the most telling aspects of the show was that every
individual featured (excluding myself) was getting paid
several hundred thousand dollars per year off the backs of
college athletes. At the same time, they were attempting
to explain why neither the kids, nor their families, should
get any of that money. The hypocrisy really sells itself in
the CBS setup, because there is no excuse for this
behavior.

My argument with the NCAA is that they have to make a
choice: They should either become purely capitalist or
purely socialist. You can't be capitalist when signing
multi-million dollar sponsorship deals and paying coaches
the salaries of movie stars, and then hide behind a
socialist agenda when players show up for their cut of the
money. A purely capitalist organization is one in which
every member of that organization has rights to pursue
revenue maximization. If endorsement deals are being
signed that use player images or player jerseys are being
sold in Wal-Mart, then the player and his family have a
right to a share of that revenue. The fundamental reality
is that basketball games don't happen without basketball
players, you simply can't get around that fact.

If a socialist agenda that focuses on the academic mission of the NCAA is to be pursued (imagine that; players going to college to actually get an education!) then these constraints should be respected and endured by everyone involved:

- Coaches have salary caps of (say), $100,000 per year.

- Players are not allowed to play games on a school night or miss class in order to play

- Any coach with a low graduation rate will be fired.

- Endorsement deals or TV rights deals would be disallowed.

While this scenario sounds like it would create a ridiculous and wasteful world, it would at least allow student athletes to actually become both students and athletes. At this point, they've only had the chance to be athlete-students.

In addition to the many arguments presented to keep athletes and their families in poverty, there are also those who simply say "If the athletes don't like the system, they should just do something else. It is their choice to join the NCAA." The problem with this argument is that the NCAA has been allowed to operate like the mafia. The cartel they have formed in collegiate athletics, were it in nearly any other industry, would have been busted up by the Justice Department long ago. The truth of the matter is that all universities across America have come together and agreed to only pay a flat wage to all of their sources of labor. The University of North Carolina, the University of Kansas and UCLA are allowed to only compensate their players with tuition, nothing more. Additionally, the formation of this cartel gives unparalleled power to the

218

NCAA to control all options the players may have. This is not allowed in other business industries.

To make the analogy more clear, imagine you are out looking for a job. The company makes you an offer of, say $35,000 per year, and you consider the offer. If you are offered $35,000 per year but know that you are worth, say, $50,000 per year, you can leave the offer at the table and go to the company across the street. But if every company in your industry has gotten together and agreed to not compete with one another, you would be forced to take $35,000 in salary. This is not the correct wage for you, because the reason you are worth $50,000 is because you would generate wealth for the company you work for. There is an extra $15,000 being "left on the table" that you cannot negotiate for, because you don't have any other options. The extra $15,000 you are worth would be shared among the companies who've all agreed to restrict your available options. That is what happens with college athletes.

I had a conversation with a friend, Richard Southall, Director of the College Sport Research Institute at the University of North Carolina, Chapel Hill. In my discussions with Richard (who is one of the most prominent college sport researchers in the world), I explained that the NCAA's exploitation of the black community is not the fault of the NCAA or its members. Part of it is the fault of the black community for not strengthening itself to challenge the exploitation.

The truth of the matter is that human beings are wired to protect our own interests. Power only respects power, and people only do the right thing when they are given an incentive to do so. If those being exploited when organizations or individuals choose to do the wrong thing refuse to come together to challenge the exploitation, then the process is going to continue.

The activities of the NCAA present yet another situation in which African-Americans continue to allow others to extract resources from our community without being challenged. The weapons to fight this dramatic economic bullying are education, awareness, courage and unity. Without putting these valuable assets in place, it is always going to be difficult for us to protect our financial assets.

Chapter 17

What Now?

As you can see, this book was not written to focus solely on money. Money is not the ends in itself. Money is the means toward liberation and empowerment. By understanding how money works in a capitalist society, how it affects our options and happiness, we can harness the power of money to achieve the social freedom and empowerment that we seek.

Money and capitalism drive America. It is how Obama got elected. It is the reason that most of us are afraid to speak up on issues that affect our lives. It is the reason for most divorces. It is the reason that we were all shaking in our boots when the economy crashed in 2008.

Black people have much to learn when it comes to managing money and harnessing its power. We can also learn how financial empowerment links back to educational achievement, so that we can create a path to success for ourselves in the 21st century. The world is getting more competitive and in some ways, the African-American is among the least prepared to survive during this time. As capitalism grips the world, we will find that the gap between the rich and the poor will grow. We will also find that some will be freer than ever, while many more will be victims of virtual enslavement. So, teach your children the value of entrepreneurship, money management and financial freedom, so they are not undermined by the flaws of global capitalism.

221

The future belongs to us if we decide to take it. This is your road map, now go out and make it happen.

About the Author

Dr. Boyce Watkins

Dr. Boyce Watkins has presented his message to millions, appearing on CNN, NBC, CBS and nearly every other major media outlet in America. He is a regular writer for AOL Black Voices and a commentator for "Keeping it Real with Rev. Al Sharpton," a nationally-syndicated radio show. He is also the founder of the Your Black World Coalition, with over 50,000 members nation-wide.

Dr. Watkins is a Finance Professor at Syracuse University, the first African American in the history of Syracuse University to ever hold the post. He earned his BA and BS degrees with a nearly perfect GPA and a triple major in Finance, Economics and Business Management from The University of Kentucky.

In college, he was selected as Freshman of the Year, and The Wall Street Journal Outstanding Graduating Senior. He then went on to earn his Master's Degree in Mathematical Statistics and his Doctorate in Financial Economics, being the only African American in the United States to earn a PhD in Finance during the year 2002.

He does a great deal of public speaking and financial research, and is also the author of *Everything You Ever Wanted to Know About College* and *Dirty Secrets of College Success* and *The Parental 411 – What Every Parent Should Know About Their Child in College*. Dr. Watkins lives in New York and spends his semesters writing, teaching and doing research.

Other Titles by Dr. Boyce Watkins

Financial Lovemaking – Merging Assets with Your Partner in Ways that Fell Good

What if George Bush Were A black Man?

Everything You Ever Wanted to Know About College – A Guide for Minority Students

Quick and Dirty Secrets of College Success – A Professor Tells It All

The Parental 411 – What Every Parent Should Know About their Child in College

Purchase online at:
www.boycewatkins.com
www.amazon.com